MY TEN COMMANDMENTS

THE SECRET OF A GOOD LIFE

Chhavi Raj Dosaj

MY TEN COMMANDMENTS: THE SECRET OF A GOOD LIFE
By Chhavi Raj Dosaj

For the monk
who changed my life.

Contents

Introduction

The Origin of This Book

Now, I seldom like to dwell on the past; however, I would like to share the story of how this book came into existence.

Before the COVID-19 pandemic, I lived a so-called "busy life", with no time to listen to my inner voice. I was constantly reacting to life rather than creating it. In the early days of the pandemic in 2020, I started getting into periods of anxiety and fear, watching the news of global distress and deaths. I felt these emotions were already there previously, but they started showing up more.

To overcome this, I regularly started visiting a national park near my home in Sydney during the early morning hours. Soon, I became fascinated with spending time sitting by myself on the top of a hill. This practice enabled an inner shift, and I started having conversations with myself.

One day, during my time there, I was thinking about how God spoke to Moses on Mount Sinai 3,500 years ago and gave him commandments to guide people on how to live. I started wondering: If God spoke to Moses now, what commandments would he give him to help people in every aspect of current life? A set of guidelines that can help people find calm in a chaotic life? From that day onwards, I started pondering about a set of internal rules that could be the secret to a good life. I spent the next two years carving out space to listen to the wisdom of the great thinkers of the past and my own. This book is the result of a personal, spiritual, philosophical, and intellectual journey that began many years ago and has taken many twists and turns since.

The journey of discovering these commandments and writing this book was a life-changing experience for me. In thinking, researching, and drafting this book, I have attained a deep peace and bliss unscathed by the outside noise that I had been missing for a long time. While writing this book, I often felt I was writing it for myself.

I hope, like it did for me, this book will help you find your true self and empower you to live a meaningful and harmonious life. The commandments in this book are universal and applicable in all situations. As Plato said, "Truths are eternal."

Acknowledgments

I am thankful to Christine Sung for helping me review this book. Many thanks to Anna Douderina and Lynly Siely for providing me with direction when I felt lost. Thanks to my family for patiently supporting me during this entire process. Many examples, stories, and anecdotes are the results of a collection from various sources over the last twenty years. Unfortunately, sources were not always noted or available; hence it became impractical to provide an accurate acknowledgment. Regardless of the source, I wish to express my gratitude to those who have contributed to this work, even though anonymously. I have remixed some old stories and introduced some new characters, making them more relatable in the present context.

Every effort has been made to give credit where it is due for the material contained herein. If inadvertently omitted, future publications will provide due credit to those brought to the author's attention.

Disclaimer

I am not a medical expert/trained professional, and the contents of this book are for informational purposes only. The content is not intended to be a substitute for professional advice, diagnosis, or treatment. Always seek the advice of your mental health professional or other qualified health providers with any questions you may have regarding your condition. Never disregard professional advice or delay seeking it because of something you have read in this book.

This book is not intended to hurt the religious sentiments of anyone. The Ten Commandments mentioned in the book are a work of fiction based on my imagination and are in no way related to the original Ten Commandments revealed to Moses by God on Mount Sinai. I have only used the word "Thou" from the original commandments, which loosely translates to "You".

Although all efforts have been made to ensure the accuracy of this book's contents, we cannot guarantee 100 percent correctness of the information contained herein. If you find any factual anomalies, grammar, or spelling errors, please send them along with your comments and suggestions to the author.

MY TEN COMMANDMENTS

THE SECRET OF A GOOD LIFE

Commandment I

Thou Should Know Yourself

Knowing yourself is the beginning of all wisdom.
— Aristotle

When the Greek philosopher Socrates was young, one of his friends asked the famous Oracle of Delphi, who the wisest person alive in Athens was. The answer he received was that it was Socrates. Yet, Socrates himself doubted the oracle's words and determined to refute it by finding a man wiser than him. He identified the wisest people of Athens and entered into debate with them in the hope of finding that he was less wise than them.

Yet, during the debates, he discovered a strange thing: most wise men pretended they knew everything. None of them were ready to accept their weaknesses or challenge their own beliefs. On the contrary, Socrates believed that the definition of true wisdom is to "know what you know but also accept what you do not know". According to him, this definition was the true way to recognize the limits of our wisdom and understanding—knowing what you truly know and what you have yet to learn.

Finally, he realized the Oracle was right as he was the only one who could look deep into himself and was prepared to admit his ignorance rather than pretend to know something he did not.

He proved his wisdom by recognizing his limits and acknowledging his failings, which others would not. As his student and philosopher Plato has him saying in *The Apology of Socrates*: "What I do not know, I do not think I know."

Socrates claimed that one of the oldest pearls of wisdom in Greek thought was 'know thyself'. This mantra, inscribed on the temple at Delphi, was meant to evoke a simple idea: Truth must be found within yourself. In an era where moral structures were being truly defined for the first time, Socrates argued that rather than uncritically accepting traditions or customary views, we have to find moral truths within. He emphasized that having self-knowledge is more important than just learning, as we are a product of natural growth emerging from within our lives. According to him, a person can only use virtue if guided by perfect knowledge and that knowledge comes from within. Only with this self-knowledge, there is right thinking and, hence, right action.

So, how can we know ourselves? Socrates got the answer to this question when he returned from fighting in the Peloponnesian War. Upon his return, he asked one of the local boys about the meaning of Sophrosyne—the Greek word for temperance or moderation and the essence of a life well lived. After a long debate, the boy's cousin suggests that the key to Sophrosyne is simple: self-awareness. Later, Socrates sums up his argument: "Only a wise person who has self-awareness will be able to examine and tell what he knows and doesn't know." For him, self-awareness is central to how we experience the world, and it can be gained by the conscious reflection of one's feelings and thoughts. Self-awareness is a constant process that never ends. It develops further and further each time with every step we take to recognize the core of our existence. And as we do so, we learn valuable lessons that we can gradually incorporate into every aspect of our life. This is one of the ways to break free from old habits and patterns that have been unconsciously directing our path in life. Once we have this self-awareness, we can reward ourselves by revealing our inherent brilliance. Chinese philosopher Lao Tzu believed that gaining self-awareness is one of the highest pursuits of life. He later wrote, "To know that one does not know is the best; not to know but to believe that one knows is a disease."

Like Socrates and Lao, we must distinguish between knowledge and true wisdom. We must understand that true wisdom can't come from accumulating factual knowledge or cramming your mind with information. Instead, it comes from a deep understanding of oneself. As the Bhagwat Gita says, "Compose yourself in stillness, draw your attention inward, and devote your mind to the self. This wisdom you seek lies within." Once we are aware of our thoughts and feelings and carefully observe our behavior in everyday incidents in human relationships, we can seek the wisdom of self-knowledge. As Lao Tzu said, "Knowing others is knowledge but knowing yourself is true wisdom."

The Illusion of Our Shadows

In his book *Republic*, Plato talks about the 'Allegory of the Cave', where a group of prisoners are sitting in a cave. These prisoners are shackled in such a position that they can only face the cave's back wall, and they are not able to see each other. A fire behind them casts the shadows of objects onto the wall. Since childhood, they have been there, so they don't know anything else. In the absence of any other experience, they accept the shadows as reality.

One day, they are suddenly set free. As these prisoners turn and face the cave entrance, at first, they are dazzled by the light and cannot see anything clearly. Once they are accustomed to the daylight, they slowly start to know the 'true' reality. Finally, they are able to look at the sun itself and realize that it is the source of the daylight that illuminates the reality all around us.

Without being aware, most of us also live a part of our lives like these prisoners, staring at a cave wall, considering the shadows to be reality. Once we realize that the source of knowledge, the sun, is not outside but lying deep within us, we can understand the true reality of life. By knowing ourselves, we are able to undo the debilitating illusions that have been laid over our majestic selves. This exercise can help us break our chains of ignorance, free ourselves from the metaphorical cave, and crawl our way into the sunlight of genuine knowledge.

There is a famous Indian parable about an elephant that wandered into a village of blind people. Not knowing what an elephant is, the blind villagers began to examine the huge animal with their hands. One man grabbed the elephant's trunk and said, "This animal is like a big snake." Another one who wrapped himself around the elephant's leg announced, "This creature is like a tree trunk." Another blind man touched the tail and said, "This feels like a rope." Another one who was able to reach the elephant's ear said, "I think it is like a hand fan." Finally, the one who placed his hand on the side of the elephant declared, "I know this animal is like a big wall."

Though all the blind people were partially right, none of them was totally correct. They identified the parts they touched accurately, yet none of them could identify the whole picture. Due to their limited perspective and unwillingness to accept the views of the others, they understood only a piece of the puzzle. Don't you think sometimes we act like these blind villagers, not prepared to accept others' opinions? Rather than denying it, we should be self-aware that there are limitations to our perspective, and we only know a piece of the big picture. You must agree that once we acknowledge and accept this reality, we will be more open and ready to learn new things to understand the whole truth.

Look into Yourself

Once a friend of philosopher Sextius visited him from another town. Sextius took him on a tour of the house. The friend was surprised to see a small room full of big mirrors before his bedroom. He asked Sextius, "What is the purpose of having this room?"

Sextius replied, "I follow a daily practice. Before I retire for my nightly rest, I sit in this room, look at myself in the mirror from each angle, and examine my entire day, measuring my deeds and words.

After that, I ask myself, 'What fault or bad habit of mine have I cured today? What cravings for bad things have I resisted? In what way am I better today than yesterday?'"

The confused friend asked, "Do you try to ignore your shortcoming during this retrospective?"

Sextius replied, "I hide nothing from myself; I pass over nothing. For why should I be afraid of any of my shortcomings when it is in my power to say, I pardon you this time but promise that you will never do that anymore?"

The friend smiled and asked, "What do you really gain from these conversations with yourself?"

"When I listen to my inner voice, I am able to know myself better and gain better knowledge of my character. The best reward of this exercise is that my mind becomes deep and free, and gives me a peaceful sleep," was the answer from Sextius.

Like philosopher Sextius, have you ever looked inward and asked, "What are my greatest faults?" If you haven't yet, there is a high chance you may be wrongly keeping the accounts of your life. Though you can see your physical faults by looking in the mirror, you can realize the deficits in your inner life only by looking within yourselves. If you ignore looking inside, it is likely that you may have high expectations for how others should treat you. But on the other hand, you may not be treating others the same way. Don't you think this is a good reason to examine your life regularly? As Socrates says, "The unexamined life is not worth living."

One of the most significant advantages humans have over other species is the power of self-evaluating and self-correction. Self-reflection is something that each of us can do with honesty to ourselves. This practice trains our mind to be aware of our thoughts, emotions, and physical impulses rather than falling victim to them. Over time, this exercise helps us be more mindful of our actions, thus enabling us to have more control over our future. This calm introspection can also help us deal with our life confidently and decisively.

Abraham Maslow once said, "A person cannot choose wisely for a life unless he dares to listen to himself, his own self, at each moment in life." This method of reflection allows the brain to pause amidst moments of chaos, and untangle and sort through observations and experiences of the past. This reflection enables us to understand ourselves in a better way and create healthier mindsets. This exercise is also helpful for our ongoing growth and development and creates better future plans. Don't you think it is important to put time aside to ask ourselves the questions that can help us choose wisely: Are the things I am doing meaningful to me? Are they really giving me contentment?

Another advantage of taking the time to listen to our hearts, mind, emotions, and reasons regularly is that we start accepting ourselves. This exercise helps us develop a friendly relationship with our inner selves. This relationship that we build with ourselves is the one that is guaranteed to last a lifetime. Remember, a true friend will lead us in the right direction, and we have to find that true friend within ourselves. As our good friend, our inner self can give us unbiased feedback about our shortcomings and our good qualities.

Do you think there is anything more admirable than discussing the day's events with your loyal friend? You may tell your inner self, "I was harsh to my friend today," your inner self may respond, "You should make apologies to him and, in the future, speak softly." You may also say, "I shouted at my younger ones and offended them," and your inner self may respond, "Next time, be mindful and think before you react in such a situation." Some days, your conversations may look like, "I helped a person," and you will hear a round of applause from your inner self for this act. Remember, these discussions can help us fully understand our strengths and weaknesses. We also get a sense of calmness after we have received warnings or praises from our secret cross-examiner.

According to the great philosopher and mathematician Pythagoras, "Never close your eyelids until you have examined the reasons behind all your actions throughout the day." Check: What have I done today? Where did I go wrong? What did I do that was unfriendly or unsocial? What have I left undone? What can I do better next time? If you practice these things thoroughly and meditate on them well, you will know yourself better and eventually start loving yourself for who you are.

Instead of Finding Fault in Others, Examine Your Faults First

Once, Jesus was going to a place to give a sermon. On the way, he saw a group of people surrounding a woman. When Jesus inquired, they said, "This woman has been caught in the act of adultery. For this sinful act, we plan to stone her till death according to the law."

They were looking to see if Jesus would justify their actions and uphold the law. Jesus replied, "Yes, I agree she has done a sinful act, and she has to be punished. Okay, go ahead and stone her. But look into yourself first; the only one who has never done any sin in his life can cast the first stone."

One by one, the people from the crowd started to disappear. Eventually, Jesus was alone with the woman. Before leaving, he told the woman, "See how now no one is left to condemn you. Go and never do any more sins."

Once Jesus acquainted people with their shortcomings, they stopped pointing fingers at others. The beauty of looking inside is that it helps us understand that nobody is perfect, including us. Kabir, a fifteenth-century Indian mystic and poet, in one of his famous poems, talks about how he failed miserably in his quest to find the most evil person in the world. In the end, when he looked into his heart, he realized there was no one worse than him. This poem is a beautiful description of our opinions about others. Don't you think that most of the time, we are busy criticizing and condemning others for their faults while ignoring our own imperfections?

So, the next time you find yourself in a situation where you are thinking about others' shortcomings, dive deep into your own self and do an honest self-analysis. This exercise may help you realize that most of the flaws we complain about in others also lie within us. We have been ignoring them due to our arrogance and wrong perceptions. It is time now to identify and work on correcting them. Once we start acknowledging them, it can help us adopt a more loving and compassionate attitude, and the whole world will start looking more beautiful. As English writer Aldous Huxley said, "There's only one part of the universe you can be certain of improving, and that is your own self."

Do you Feel 'At Home' with Yourself?

One day Confucius asked four of his students about their aspirations. The first one replied hastily, "I want to run a big country with a vast army, which is caught between two large kingdoms. In less than three years, not only will I tackle the other kingdoms, but I will solve all the problems within the country."

Confucius smiled at him and asked the second one the same question. The second one said, "I want to govern a small state, and after three years, I will be able to give the common people enough food to eat and clothes to wear."

The third one said, "I don't have the ambition to rule a country, but I am happy to work as a minor official who can participate in the state rituals and meetings."

When the master asked the last one who was busy playing his musical string instrument, he waited for the sound of the music to fade gradually. Then he said calmly, "I desire to go and bask in the spring breeze at the side of the river with friends and come home singing songs. I want to get close to nature to get peace for my inner heart and cleanse myself. This is all I want."

When Confucius heard his aspiration to connect with himself, he replied, "I am with you!"

Every one of us has personal goals, but in the hurried endless, repeated cycles of rhythms of work, we seldom take time and space to pay attention and listen to our inner hearts. On the material level, a happy life is no more than a series of goals to be reached. Still, true peace and stability come when we feel connected with ourselves.

Have you noticed that we all tend to spend too much time looking at the outside world and too little looking within our hearts? However, the truth is, the secret to life is to find peace within us. While we are busy listening to the voice of the outside world, we often muffle the voice of our own spirit. Having big plans or grand ambitions is not wrong, but first, we need to understand the yearning of our own hearts. In order to listen to our inner voice, we need to slow down and crave some time to start the journey of self-discovery. Once we go on an inner journey, we can hear our wisdom and re-discover what we already know. In most indigenous cultures, nature is considered our self-reflection. Therefore, spending time with nature can help us listen to our inner voice.

Roman emperor Marcus Aurelius once wrote, "For nowhere can you find a more peaceful and less busy retreat than in your own soul. Treat yourself often to this retreat and be renewed." Don't you think that unless we have a feeling of being 'at home' with ourselves, of being able to rest and relax within, we will not be at home anywhere? Once we have found a loving foundation within, we can more easily remain grounded, stable, and unshakeable in any situation.

In his book, *The Tao Made Easy*, Allan Cohen writes that from infancy we are taught that outsiders know more than you and how you should live your life. Parents, elders, siblings, teachers, and the government are all smarter than you, and if you want to be happy and successful, you must listen to what they tell you to do. Eventually, each of us comes to the point where we realize that how we were taught to live is not the way we were born to live. Sometimes, we are afraid to face ourselves as we believe we will find pain and darkness. Therefore, we create an endless stream of errands, tasks, obligations, problems, dramas, and emergencies to keep us preoccupied with the outer world. If you are also doing the same, take time to retreat, to reclaim your soul; all outward journeys ultimately lead inward, where real answers live. The fool searches in the outer world; the master goes within.

Conclusion

In one of the episodes of *Star Trek*, former captain and admiral Jean-Luc Picard is asked, "Have you ever been a stranger to yourself?" Picard replies, "Many, many times." I am sure you would have felt the same thing many times despite your best efforts and intentions. In our pursuit to continually connect with others, we often become disconnected with ourselves. When this happens regularly, we experience that our actions, thoughts, and perceptions differ from our views. A gap between who we are and how we live our lives causes an increased level of fear, frustration, conflicts, and depression. If we take the time to look inside, we will find that wisdom is always there waiting to talk to us and show us another way. The answers are in here; we just need to draw them forth.

In one of my favorite movies, *The Matrix*, Neo, doubtful of his superhuman abilities, goes to the Oracle to find out whether he is "The One" who has the power to change the world. Instead of giving a straight answer, the Oracle refers to a Latin saying 'know thyself' on her wall. Neo leaves the room, still not able to believe in himself. Later, when he reawakens in the Matrix, he accepts his true nature and finds himself a real match for his enemies. Believing in himself and his powers was the most important part of being "The One". As the Oracle said, believing in yourself is like being in love, nobody can tell you, you just know it.

Like Neo, to know your true potential, you also need to 'look into yourself'. This exercise requires complete transparency, like being true to yourself. For long, you may have looked at others and accepted yourselves as the reflection in their eyes, ignoring your true personality. Think, for a while: Is this why you have masked your values and true potential? If you want to reclaim it back and recognize and embrace your individuality and real powers, YOU NEED TO KNOW YOURSELF. Once you embrace this journey, you will have the power and creative ability to write your own life story. Keep making effort to stay on the right path. We all have a mirror in our hearts; now is the time to see our true reflection. Based on the reflection, the perspectives and metaphors we choose will truly define us. Carl Jung once said, "Those who look outside dream, those who look inside awaken."

In his book, *Analects*, Confucius says that once we are mature, we need to 'take a stand'. This is the time to introspect, so we can evaluate our life against our internal standards, not through external social standards. Most of the time, we are waiting for external sources to give us direction in life, forgetting we have an inbuild GPS inside which is waiting to guide us. All the answers and directions are inside, but we don't dare to ask ourselves. Awaken yourself with the great words of Sufi mystic Rumi,

"You are the divine word,
you mirror the majesty of the king.
All the world is contained in you.
What you are seeking is within."

Keys to Knowing Yourself

➢ Try to use this affirmation first thing in the morning—"I will be my best friend today."

➢ Every night, like a friend, do a self-evaluation of your everyday events by asking the following questions:

- o Were you being disrespectful to others?
- o Were you ignoring others' feelings?
- o What are the areas to improve upon?
- o What have you done great today, for which you feel proud?

➢ If you find that you have treated people in a way you would not like to be treated, with a sincere heart, without any justification, apologize to these people.

➢ This everyday self-appraisal will assess your strengths and weakness, giving you new insights about yourself.

➢ Work on a plan to correct your faults and bad habits to be a better person.

➢ Always remember, we know only the partial truth, so respect others' perspectives and always be eager to learn new things.

➢ Work on making yourself your BFF (best friend forever) with whom you are always upfront. Work toward this goal every day.

➢ Take time to connect with yourself; remember it is a lifelong journey.

➢ The most important thing to learn in life is to 'know how to live', which is something only we can teach ourselves.

Commandment II

Thou Shall Renounce Anger

Anger causes delusion,
delusion confuses thinking,
and confused thinking corrupts reasoning.
Thereafter arises total ruination of a person.
– Bhagavad Gita

In the great Indian epic Mahabharat, the five Pandava brothers, after losing their kingdom in the game of dice, were exiled to the forest for twelve years. One day, in the course of their wandering, they were faced with dire thirst. One by one, they sought to take water from a lake that was guarded by a sprite. The sprite had a condition that each of them must answer his questions before taking the water. The younger four brothers refused to follow the sprite's condition and in turn each of them perished.

At last, the eldest and wisest of the five, Yudhishthira, agreed to answer the questions. The sprite is delighted with his answers and rewards him with water and revives his deceased brothers.

A vitally insightful answer he provides is to the sprite's first question,

"Who is the greatest enemy of human beings?"

Yudhishthira's prompt answer was "**Their own uncontrolled anger.**"

Do you think that answer still holds today when humans have made tremendous progress in every aspect of life? Whether you agree or disagree, I am sure you have become victim to your own anger at some point in life. Some of us are temporary victims, and some continue to be permanent victims of this emotion, suffering the tragedy it brings to our lives.

According to the Bhagavad Gita, "Our mind is our best friend and our worst enemy." When our mind succumbs to anger, we become our own enemy. That is why uncontrolled anger is the biggest obstacle to our happiness. In a fit of rage, we can even hurt our dearest ones and destroy the good impressions they have of us, which have been acquired through years of effort, in an instant. Before we can go deeper into this subject, it is necessary to understand the origin and purpose of this emotion.

Anger is a natural emotion that originates when an event in life causes different levels of frustration. It can be from pain, displeasure, or when someone is trying to invade our personal space. It also happens when our beliefs or ways of thinking are challenged or in response to stress or opposition. It is inescapable, and like any other emotion, it provides an important clue to our current situation. Anger itself is not bad, evil, destructive, or sinful as it helps us recognize and warns us when something is wrong. Anger is actually essential to a healthy personality; someone who never feels anger is not always going to do the right thing and will, therefore, not achieve happiness. Though this emotion in its true form lasts for only a few minutes, the rest of the experience has to do with the wounds and stories we tell ourselves. Still, rather than processing anger in a healthy way, most of us get carried away by this emotion and later blame anger for our wrongdoings.

In the early 2000s, I moved to the USA, and one day, while cooking, the smoke alarm went off (I realized later that these smoke alarms are pretty allergic to Indian cooking). In India, most houses don't have smoke alarms, so this irritating noise was something new for me. I panicked, trying to figure out what had gone wrong. My initial thought was that the whole apartment was probably on fire, the lift won't be working, and I might have to jump from the window to save myself. Luckily, my neighbor came out and explained why the alarm started and how to diffuse it. Our anger is pretty much like the smoke alarm, which starts beeping to indicate that something needs attention. But rather than trying to find the root cause to process it firmly and positively, we panic and therefore take the wrong steps to get out of this emotion.

Most reasons for awakening this emotion, like the smoke detector, are false alarms. Some petty causes that are laughable in hindsight later. But once this emotion has taken control of our mind, the inner peace vanishes in a moment, and then we don't care whether it is a true or false alarm. Eventually, our mind becomes an erupting volcano ready to melt even the hardest of rocks.

We all know the evil effects of uncontrolled anger. That is why the wise sometimes calls it a 'period of short madness'. There are numerous examples in history in which even the most righteous of men ordered people to be slaughtered, cities to be sacked, and houses to be burned due to their bursts of rage. Even today, anger is one of the main reasons for domestic violence and divorce. When anger becomes the second nature of a person, the physical health and stability of the mind suffer badly. When anger becomes a part of our personality, everyone tries to avoid us. Thus, our families, friendships, and personal and professional prospects suffer. Therefore, don't let your anger define you. Renounce it so people can see your true self and appreciate your good qualities. Renouncing your anger is not about suppressing or hiding this emotion. Instead, it is about acknowledging the emotion, reflecting on what caused it, and redirecting it for our own good. It is also about focusing our efforts on what is under our control rather than wasting them on what is not under our control.

The One Who Is Not Able to Control Anger Always Regrets His Action

The Roman Emperor Hadrian had a violent temper tantrum one day because an unlucky slave did something to annoy him. Hadrian was writing at the time and in a moment of madness, he stabbed the slave in the eye with his pen, blinding him.

Later, when Hadrian calmed down and came to his senses, he felt highly ashamed of himself. He summoned the slave, apologized for this horrific act, and asked what he could do to make amends.

The slave was silent for quite a long time but eventually found the courage to speak frankly to the emperor: "All I want," he said, "is my eye back."

That was something even an emperor could not grant him. Although our anger may sometimes be fleeting, the harm done by it can be permanent.

Do you remember a time when you felt pity in the same way as Emperor Hadrian because of your anger? You are not alone as it happens to all of us; we do and say things that we really don't mean under the influence of anger. Later, when we realize it is impossible to reverse these actions, we start feeling bad about ourselves. According to Seneca, other people's actions might harm us physically and damage our property or reputation; however, uncontrolled anger injures our moral character. Therefore, it hurts us much more profoundly than any other person's actions.

Like the Emperor, the first thing that happens to us when we are angry is that we forget the lessons of wisdom we have learned so far; we become deaf to both reason and advice. After that, we lose control over our own thoughts and emotions. At this time, we are incapable of perceiving things in their actual perspective and, therefore, fail to distinguish between right and wrong. As the wise say, "If he has anger in his heart, what further enemy he needs."

This doesn't mean that we have no control over our anger. One of the main reasons humans are superior to animals is because we have the power of self-control. We have the power to control our emotions, but often, we see ourselves mastered by our own emotions. It is not all our fault, as one of life's greatest tragedies is that we are seldom taught how to manage anger or other emotions when we are young.

Rather than teaching children how to control their anger, parents and teachers vent it onto them when they are frustrated. When the children see their role models following these patterns of response to anger, they pick it up from them. Later they start repeating the same pattern when they themselves are angry. If we can control our anger better, there is a good chance we can teach the same to our future generations.

Let's talk about how we can control our anger. The first step toward anger management is to be conscious of our anger. Only when we are conscious of our feelings, do we have the power to control them. The second step is to defer our response as 'delaying is one the best antidotes to anger'. As anger is an eroding emotion, we can have better judgment if we take the time to think first. This restraint is not the same as storing our anger, but it is a way to let the anger subside. Sometimes, you may have to fight hard to restrain yourself, and if you find you cannot conquer anger, do not let it conquer you. Remember that when you treat your rage, you are both the patient as well as the physician. The best form of restraining is to take a few deep breaths. Still, some prefer drinking a glass of water, taking a brisk walk, running, or jogging to drop the additional energy created by anger. Once you spend that energy, your anger will automatically subside.

As Seneca explains in his book *On Anger*, no one really thinks to postpone their anger, yet delay is one of the best remedies for it. The delay allows us time to clear the cloud that has darkened the mind. Over time this passion becomes lighter and may vanish altogether in many cases. Even if you gain nothing by your adjournment, the decision you will take after the gap results from mature deliberation, not anger.

Seneca further advises that if you are unable to resist anger and cast an angry look, count to ten before you open your mouth to lash out those angry words. If angry words have escaped your lips and you could not resist them, count to one hundred before raising your hands to strike the person. But, if everything fails and you hit the person, please do not delay apologizing with all sincerity.

After we have taken a reasonable delay, the third step is to analyze the situation rationally. This will help us to find out why we are feeling angry and think about what we should do constructively.

Don't Stop Hissing

One day, an old wise sage was passing through a village. The villagers told him they were terrified of a violent snake living in a burrow on their way to the fields. The snake would bite anyone who travels on that path. The sage sought out the snake through his magical power and told him not to bite the villagers.

The snake decided to follow the instructions of the sage and was no longer vicious. However, taking advantage of the snake's peaceful state, some mischievous people occasionally started annoying him by throwing twigs and small stones at his burrow.

A few days later, when the sage returned from his journey, he found the snake looking weak and pale. His poor state saddened the sage. "What happened?" he asked.

"As people noticed that I no longer bite them, they started taking advantage of me. They often annoy me, and they have ruined my burrow. I have lost my sleep and peace while trying to suppress my anger."

The sage replied, "Fool! I have told you not to express your anger by biting, but why didn't you express your anger by hissing!"

We have all seen actions resulting from anger are often wrong and should be avoided at all costs. Still, like the snake, we will labor under a sense of resentment if we keep silent and don't do anything. This resentment, like a parasite, slowly decays the body in which it dwells. As Seneca said, "Anger is an acid that can do more harm to the vessel in which it is stored than to anything on which it is poured." As holding the anger can bring more harm to you, it is necessary to admit your anger to yourself and the actual perpetrator. This is the best way to release and process this emotion safely.

There is also a good chance that if we do not express our anger towards the perpetrator, we may vent it on others later. Thus, the ill feeling proliferates! Since our anger is concealed, nobody tries to soothe us, which can then take the form of bitterness. If positive steps are not taken, the heaviness of all that injustice and resentment begins to show in our overall personality. Rather than carrying these feelings forever, we need to put them down. The healthy way of handling that anger is to tell (hissing) our feeling to the person who has wronged us in a polite and honest way. We should never confront wrong done to us with ill will and spite but in a loving way to seek a healthy resolution. Always remember, suppressing feelings like anger is not good. These feelings need to be expressed but in a restrained and balanced way; only then can we be in harmony with ourselves.

When we feel anger towards someone or something, most of the hate for that person or situation is due to our own exaggeration.

So, we need to bring calmness before we can decide whether it is valid anger or not. After that, we need to analyze and evaluate the seriousness of the issue. Our tone and response should then be based on that evaluation. The more serious the issue, the more strongly we should express it. Also, we need to remember that we are sharing our feelings objectively. Take the situation of someone trying to bully you. This is an example of valid anger and a serious issue; therefore, we must take suitable action. After a delay, you must firmly express your feelings to the person who has caused it. Say "I feel angry when you bully me," rather than saying, "You are a bully."

Another situation can be during a flight when someone in the front is trying to crush their seat towards your knees. In this case, if you don't express your feelings, you will keep getting agitated. Still, it is a light issue as there is a good chance that the person isn't deliberately set out to irritate you; it's just that they haven't thought about you as much as their comfort. Therefore, we must express our feelings about the legitimacy of one's position in a light tone. Say "Excuse me, I am sure you don't realize, but the back of your seat is squashing my knees," rather than saying, "Move your seat, don't you see it is hurting me?" Once we healthily express anger, there is a good chance our anger will settle positively. This will also open room for a positive dialog and thus a healthy resolution.

You Should Know Which Battles to Fight

One day, a man visited a sage living on a city's outskirts. He told the sage that he often gets provoked when other people throw their anger at him. In these situations, he often loses his temper and hurts them back with words. He was looking for some advice to control his anger in these situations.

As the sage was going to the city, he asked him to accompany him so they could discuss this problem in detail.

As they progressed to the city, they saw a group of dogs approaching an elephant. The dogs soon started barking, but the elephant, as joyful as before, kept walking. The elephant did not even stand and look at the dogs. It was as if he had not heard them. The dogs kept a distance, followed the elephant, and barked with their full strength but the elephant kept walking at the same pace. Finally, the dogs stopped barking.

The sage said, "Learn to be a wise elephant; when others try to irritate you with their words, do not pay attention, just ignore them, and they will stop soon. Do not try to tame the barking dogs by getting into a fight with them. You have it within your power to completely tune them out by being an elephant that keeps walking while the dogs are barking."

I am sure you will agree that anger is contagious like most other emotions; it is easy to get angry in the presence of another angry person. Most anger felt and exhibited by one person towards another stirs additional anger as a counter-response like a chain reaction. If we try to counter anger with anger, it spreads fast like wildfire. Therefore, it is important to act like the wise elephant. This strategy is quite effective when dealing with the rage of strangers or people outside your immediate circle. When such situations arise, the best response to an angry person is to ignore them and walk away. Arguing with a rude person only offers them more opportunities to be rude. On the one hand, we don't have control over the anger of others, but on the other hand, we can do our best to prevent our own anger.

Whenever you find yourself in the company of someone who provokes you to lose your temper, don't try to soothe them with your words. It is better to turn away and wait for a later opportunity when they are in a calm state. In real life, if you see a mad bull on the path, what will be your best strategy to handle it? I am sure you will try to avoid him at any cost. In the same way, if you were driving and unnecessarily honked at by another driver or confronted by an angry stranger, turn away from it. Another example can be when you see provocative remarks on social media by an internet troll or online bully. Don't give them any attention; let them starve, waiting for a reaction. You can always act like the wise elephant in these situations by completely ignoring these barking dogs. In the long term, you will find that it is always better to avoid these situations rather than get into an argument to prove who is right or wrong.

Forgiving can relieve you from the burden of anger

One morning, a hunter found that a snake had killed his young son. The hunter raged in anger, went out and caught the snake, and brought it to his wife who was grieving in sorrow. The snake was all trussed up with string so that it could not move.

"Here is the culprit!" exclaimed the father raging in anger, "I will hack it to pieces! I will make him suffer for our pain!"

"Let the snake go," said the wife. "Killing it will not bring back my boy, and you will only incur sin upon yourself by doing so."

The hunter said, "Only revenge can bring comfort to my anger, so I have to kill him."

After the wife grew tired of arguing with the hunter, she said, "I have a small request; please kill this snake only after we finish the final rites of our son." The hunter agreed, and for the next few hours, they were both weeping together while giving a final farewell to their son.

After the rites, the hunter said to his wife, "I have killed so many animals so far, now I can understand the pain I have caused to them and their families. I cannot do that anymore. I don't have the strength to kill this snake."

The wife replied, "I knew that you were thinking about revenge under the influence of anger. This is the reason I was trying to prolong the execution. You are right: only forgiveness can now help us heal the pain."

The hunter finally found comfort in this thought and let the snake go. It was the act of forgiveness that helped the family overcome the pain and bitterness of sorrow.

We may never face such an extreme situation as the hunter in real life. Nevertheless, for some reason, we all hold on to anger or resentment towards family members or former friends when we cannot express the emotion positively. Over time, this resentment turns into bitterness, and we start thinking that only revenge can cease this feeling. The truth is that carrying this feeling could lead to more unhappiness in the long run. In the islands of the South Pacific, people believed that if you held onto resentment for some time, sickness would come. The people there believe that secrecy is what gives power to this sickness. The therapy to counter this sickness is admitting it and then expressing it politely or forgiving it. Therefore, whenever expressing or suppressing anger is not solving the problem, we must acknowledge and then use the virtues of forgiveness, patience, and forbearance to cease this bitterness. Real virtue is not in taking revenge but in forgiving the enemies.

Forgiveness acts like magic by providing an instant and lasting solution to many of our problems, including resentment and bitterness. Forgiveness has its own reward. It benefits the forgiver more than the forgiven. Instead of waiting for an apology from the person who has done wrong, we should forgive, let it go, and move on. If we don't forgive people, they will be with us 24 hours a day and will fuel our anger more; therefore, forgive and be free!

Have you ever observed that anger can alter the state of mind and cause temporary madness? Thus, when people are out of control in anger, they can sometimes act like mad or drunk people. There is a gap between their feelings for you and what they express under the influence of rage. Therefore, it is best to consider the situation and forgive them as they are just the actors speaking their part in the direction of anger. It is also necessary to understand people's situations before we decide on our actions. If you see your parents or partner coming home after a difficult day in the office and showing signs of anger, give them some concessions. Whether we decide to forgive and reconcile or to condemn or ignore, we can ask ourselves the simple question, "Which path is taking me to happiness?" Also, at regular intervals, talk to your family and friends and ask for forgiveness; it may happen that our actions have caused resentment in them as well.

To settle any anger that remains in the heart, every night before you retire, do a stocktaking of the day's events. Whosoever has angered you, take that person's name and say, 'I forgive you!' Free from all resentments, you will get a peaceful night's sleep. One of my friends uses a ritual where he writes a letter to the person whom he has resentment towards. In the letter, he will detail all the pain it has caused; the letter will end with the phrase "I forgive you" with his signature and date. But instead of mailing it, he will burn it in his fireplace. Watching it burn helps him release any unsettled anger. At the end of the day, use whatever strategy you wish to, but don't allow your anger to stay in your mind for a long time. The longer it lasts, the stronger and harder it becomes, and therefore more immense the harm. A wise person will not allow anger to stay in their mind for more than a few moments, yet only fools hold their anger until they die. Sometimes it is worth learning from children and animals—watch how their anger vanishes in a moment.

When Your Shoe Bites, Don't Bite It Back

Around 500 BC, the great Persian king Cyrus was hurrying to lay siege upon Babylon. During his expedition, he came across a river that was not safe to cross, even during the summer heat.

In a hurry, he ordered his army to cross the river. Suddenly, one of the white horses that drew the royal chariot was washed away. This loss moved the king into a violent rage. He threatened that he would weaken the river so much that, in the future, people would be able to cross it easily without ever getting their knees wet.

Having made this threat, he postponed his expedition against Babylon. He ordered all the resources of his army to devote to this project. His entire army spent the whole summer working there, creating channels on each side of the river. Finally, the riverbed was dry as the waters flowed through other channels.

But due to his madness, by getting angry at a river, he lost his aim. His army wasted their valuable time and eventually missed the great opportunity by falling upon their enemies unprepared.

Don't you agree these are examples of unjustified or invalid anger? Isn't it foolish to get angry and waste valuable energy on things beyond our control? Not only do we lose the aim of our life, but we divert our efforts and time to do unnecessary things. When we experience this type of anger, we must take steps to deal with the feelings they produce. We must teach ourselves to calm down as no one else is responsible for these feelings.

Once, a small boy got angry because he was drenched by the rain. He used all his energy to spit at the sky but ended up having the spit fall back on his face. Can you imagine the roaring anger of this young boy? We often behave the same as this boy and receive the same consequence of raising our temper on occasions not in our control. Even when we feel angry about our past mistakes where we acted foolishly or carelessly, we behave like the small boy by punishing ourselves.

One of the tools that can counter the tide of anger into a calming wave of peace is your sixth sense—the sense of humor. The wise use of humor is the best way to get rid of an angry face and to soothe your mind and sometimes the minds of others. If you find yourself in a tense situation, even if a negative response appears warranted, using humor where appropriate will often endear you to others. During my early days on the job, one of my colleagues used to use humor at its best to counter anger. Whenever he made a mistake in his work, he would go to the washroom and make funny faces looking into the mirror instead of getting angry at himself.

Even President Lincoln used humor when someone made the disparaging remark that he was "two-faced." He replied without being slightly offended, "I leave it to my audience. Do you think I'd wear this one if I had another face?" Socrates often used humor to calm the situation and his anger. Once, his wife abused him, and later, while he was sitting on the doorstep, she poured a bucket of water on his head. Without getting irritated, Socrates joined the passers-by in their laughter and remarked, "After thunder comes rain."

Prepare Well for Your Encounter with Anger

Emperor Ashoka was an Indian ruler around 200 BC. He executed many of his stepbrothers to ascend to the throne of the great Maurya dynasty. He was known for his short temper during the early years of his reign. All his palace officials were afraid of him because of his bad temperament. Many of his officials were executed or sent to prison for minor mistakes.

One day, while sitting on his throne, he saw a young monk passing by his palace. Somehow Ashoka found the monk fascinating and asked the guards to call him inside. Once inside, Ashoka asked for his introduction. The young monk smiled and replied I am Nigrodha, son of your elder brother Sushma.

Ashoka was shocked because he had killed his elder brother Sushma by pushing him into a hot coal pit during the succession war. However, the monk's face was calm and composed, with no sign of anger or hatred towards Ashoka.

"Are you not angry with me? Don't you have any feelings of revenge?" the emperor asked the boy cautiously.

The young monk replied, "I visualized this meeting a long time back and prepared for this occasion. Initially, my passion used to be provoked, but then I learned how to subsidize them with calmness. I have attained peace with practice, and anger is no longer my companion."

Ashoka got down from his throne, hugged him, and asked him to take any seat in the court. The monk looked around but did not find any empty seat, so he walked up to Ashoka's throne and sat on it.

Everybody was shocked as the punishment for sitting in the emperor's seat was death during that time. Still, surprisingly, in the monk's company, Ashoka did not feel anger and followed him back to his throne. Instead of punishing him, both sat on the same throne and talked about the way to attain peace and calmness.

This meeting was a turning point in the life of Ashoka. Afterwards, he decided to follow the path of non-violence and peace.

Like the Buddhist monk, do you think you can still remain calm in a situation that warrants anger? One of the best anger management plans involves telling yourself a mantra every morning, "Today, I have made a choice to control my anger with calmness." Then try to review all occasions that may occur during the course of the day, both favorable and unfavorable, and visualize the emotions they may provoke.

Once you are aware of the emotions, prepare beforehand to stifle them at the very point of inception without allowing them to control you. This plan also involves creating obstacles in the path of situations or environments that can make you feel angry. If it still happens, then remind yourself about the mantra of calmness to keep your mind stable during these encounters. This exercise will help you bear the most sudden and violent anger shocks with the calmness of your mind. Over time, you will be able to handle anger peacefully, even in unprepared situations.

Once you start using this plan, at the end of every day, you should also self-examine yourself and how you have fared with your anger management plan. In which situation do you fare better, in which do you fail, and how do you improve going forward? Anger will cease and become gentler if it knows it will have to appear before the judgment seat daily.

Calmness is Contagious

During the Vietnamese war, there was a fight to control a strategically important road. There were American soldiers on the one side of the road and Vietnamese fighters on the other side. As heavy firing was going on, nobody was able to use the road.

Suddenly, both sides saw a group of Buddhist monks crossing the road. Even after hearing the firing sound, they had not changed their path. They kept walking peacefully at the same pace as if nothing had happened.

The Vietnamese immediately stopped firing; the American soldiers soon followed them. Both sides watched the monks calmly crossing the road.

After the Buddhist monks safely passed the road, neither party started firing. Until the evening, that place had the same calmness and peace. It was looking like neither side was interested in fighting anymore.

Many of the American soldiers later recalled that peaceful moment. At that moment, most of them thought profoundly of leaving the fight and returning home to live a peaceful life.

Do you think, like anger, calmness is also contagious? Unknowingly, many of us believe that our response to anger has been a part of us since birth, but we miss an important point that most of the things we learn in life are from mirroring others. Research has shown that children learn their very first ways of life from imitating what other humans do. In the same way, most habits, including our response to anger, is copied from those we associate with. Without our knowledge, we have picked up our anger management responses from our surroundings, parents, siblings, teachers, and colleagues. We are like the little toddlers who learn to speak even though they have not learned it from teachers–but because they are surrounded by those who know how to speak. Irrespective of how, when, and from whom we have picked this, we all have the power to change ourselves and manage anger in a better way.

Once, a boy was raised at the Greek philosopher Plato's house. Later, he went back to live with his parents. One day, on seeing his father shouting with anger, he said, "I never saw anyone at Plato's house act like that." But very soon, he learned to imitate his father sooner than he learned to imitate Plato. This is one of the reasons we must try to avoid the company of people who quickly lose their cool and surround ourselves with calm people. The person who keeps the company of these quiet people is improved by their example and slowly become like them. It may be challenging to disconnect from people we may hold dear. Still, if they are bringing out the worst in us, either we need to have an open discussion with them or prioritize ourselves. Also, if we know that calmness is contagious, shouldn't we use this virtue often in front of our children and family?

Know What to Reject and What to Accept in Life

One day, Buddha was giving a lecture in a small village. A rude and angry person who belonged to another group of believers walked in. He started insulting Buddha and said, "You are a stupid and fake teacher. You have no right to teach others."

When Buddha did not reply, he continued saying bad words to him. Still, Buddha remained calm the whole time and did not say a word. The person got angrier, and he continued shouting until he was tired and frustrated in the end.

After he was done, Buddha gave a gentle smile and asked, "Tell me, if you buy a gift for someone and if that person does not take it, to whom does the gift belong?"

This question surprised the person, and he answered, "It belongs to me because I bought the gift." Buddha smiled and said, "That's right. It is exactly the same with your anger. You brought the gift of anger to me, but I did not get angry. Therefore, the anger falls back on you. All you have done is hurt yourself."

The person understood the meaning of Buddha's teaching and later became his follower.

In life, whatever we do, it is impossible to control others or our circumstances. But it is always in our power to stay calm. Like Buddha, rather than reacting with anger to win the argument, we can consider ourselves peacemakers by reminding ourselves, "Do what you will; you are too weak to disturb my calmness." Think of this as an exam to test your patience and rejoice as a winner by not getting angry.

As Seneca said, "The man who is not angry remains unshaken by an insult. In contrast, the angry one has been moved by it." Not reacting to angry words shows that you have a great mind that cannot be disturbed by an insult. In contrast, reacting to an angry word is an admission that you have been hurt. As Epictetus said, "Any person capable of angering you becomes your master. He can anger you only when you permit yourself to be disturbed by him." He later said, "If a person gave your body to some passerby, you'd be furious. Yet we so easily hand our mind over to other people, letting them get inside our head."

According to Marcus Aurelius, the best answer to anger is silence. According to him, there is little value in using words to soothe an angry person who is subsiding of their own accord. This approach will not only help in making that person's anger end quicker, but also prevent a relapse in the future.

In dealing with other people's anger, 'compassion' is a much better response than anger itself. Epictetus once said, "Pity the person who cannot control their anger instead of hating them." He further said that the best way to deal with angry people is to ask yourself, "Do you wish to help them? Then show them, by your own example." A person who can forestall anger and not react to an angry man is like a physician to both himself and the angry man. Being compassionate and not acting as a reflection of the angry person also opens the door to positive dialogue and interaction.

Conclusion

In *Master Your Emotions*, Thibaut Meurisse writes that we need to constantly remind ourselves that our emotions are not us; we are beyond our emotions. They come and go, but we always stay. We are not sad, depressed, jealous, or angry; we just witness these emotions. Our emotions are there to guide us, so we should not cling to them as our existence doesn't depend on them.

The SOS (Standby, Observe, and Steer) technique used during meditation can be used effectively to control our emotions, especially anger. Next time you are angry, try to use this technique:

1) **Standby**: Take a few deep breaths and pause without reacting quickly to the situation. Try to go into Standby mode by repeating to yourself, "I am feeling anger now." Once you notice it is just a feeling, it can help you detach from these angry emotions. If you know that these emotions are coming from other people's actions, tell yourself, "The one who angers me controls me," to detach you from that person. Once you know you are in Standby mode, try to go into the next mode.

2) **Observe**: Observe your feelings. Figure out what is driving you mad. Are you trying to exaggerate the situation? Observe any other thoughts that are trying to fuel your anger. Once you are able to observe clearly, go to the next step.

3) **Steer**: Repeat the affirmation or mantra, "I have the virtue of calmness to control my anger." This mantra will help you to steer your thoughts and help release these angry emotions. Alternatively, you can use any other personal affirmation to help you release this emotion. Now, try to think clearly about the situation and take appropriate action.

In most cases, this technique can help diffuse and release your anger. Initially, going into standby mode will be difficult as we generally react to situations. Still, with practice, you can use this technique effectively and remain calm in any situation. Remember, an angry mind is like a small kid who has taken a kitchen knife, believing it is a toy to play with. If we try to take it forcefully, the child can be hurt. Instead, if we offer another toy to him, he will forget the knife and take the new toy to play with. In the same way, we should never forcefully try to suppress our anger but instead offer new toys in the form of calmness and peace to the mind.

Regular retrospection in life is also necessary for better anger management. One of the main reasons for our anger is that we have set very high expectations for others and how our lives carry out. If things don't go according to our plan or people don't behave as we want, we get irritated. We need to regularly re-evaluate how we understand and see life to keep fewer expectations from others and ourselves. In that case, there is a good chance we won't feel anger in itself. According to Marcus Aurelius, it is naive and foolish to expect people to be perfect and act rationally at all times. When someone acts in an objectionable way, we should tell ourselves that it is to be expected from time to time. It is merely a part of life. Acting less shocked makes it easier to respond calmly and rationally to events that might otherwise make us feel enraged and offended.

When we feel angry with a person, we need to broaden our perspective and look beyond the behavior that is annoying us. Think of love or good things about the person you are mad at. We should also try to understand their actions better by placing them in a broader context. This can help us dilute our feelings of anger. We all have positive qualities like patience, tolerance, empathy, and kindness, which we can use to deal more constructively with difficult people. Reminding ourselves of these positive qualities and contemplating how they can be applied can help us find an alternative to anger and a better way of coping.

We also need to understand better what needs our anger meets for us. Is it the power? A way to feel significant? Be heard or seen? Or perhaps a way to release emotions we are not yet mature enough to process? We need to understand how we can meet these needs better rather than see the short-term advantages of anger. Take the example of the angry mother who thinks that her children are obeying her because of her angry behavior. She completely ignores the fact that she will lose their respect once they grow up. Eventually, her children will also inherit her angry behavior.

Finally, however we manage our anger, we need to take full responsibility for it rather than blaming others. Chinese mystic, Chuang Tzu uses the concept of the empty boat to help us in self-realization and thus better anger management. Imagine a man is crossing a river and an empty boat collides with his skiff; he will not feel anger even though he is a bad-tempered man. But if he sees a man in the boat, he will be enraged and start shouting at him to steer clear. If the shout is not heard, he will shout again and again and eventually begin cursing. And all because there is somebody on the boat. Therefore, whenever you encounter someone who irritates or provokes anger in you, remind yourself, "The other person is merely an empty boat. The anger is within me."

Keys for Renouncing Anger

➢ Accept that uncontrolled anger is one of your worst enemies. Unless you name your enemy, you cannot overcome it.

➢ Acknowledging that you get angry is the first step towards the journey. Seek out your family members most affected by your anger and tell them that you are working on this and would need their help.

➢ Remember, you cannot always beat anger, but you can make yourself so strong that your rage cannot win over you easily. Your recovery from anger shows your true strength.

➢ Make a rule every morning to tell yourself: "My peace does not lie at the mercy of others." Then in a calm state, review and prepare for all the occasions throughout the course of the day where your anger can burst.

➢ Look out for conditions that fuel your anger. People often get angry when they have had less sleep, are tired, hungry, or thirsty, or are under the influence of alcohol. Try to avoid these situations as best you can.

➢ Do a self-examination every evening of how you reacted to various situations throughout the day. Check if your ego is fueling your anger by delighting in finding others' faults and completely ignoring your own.

➢ If you fail to overcome anger, do not treat yourself too harshly, be gentle to yourself. It will take a lot of practice to control anger.

➢ Showing compassion to an angry person also applies when you are mad at yourself.

Commandment III

Thou Should Be Kind to Yourself

Be kind to yourself first,
only then can you be kind to others.

Once, a wise man traveling through a deep forest was confronted by a bandit. The wise man was frightened as the bandit looked hideous with torn clothes, a big beard, and black teeth. He smelled like he had not taken a bath for a long time. The bandit said, "I rule this forest; give me whatever you have and be ready to meet death." The wise man handed over all his valuable things without uttering a word. Before the bandit was about to kill him, he asked if the man had any last wishes.

The wise man mumbled, "O, Lord of the jungle, I was always fascinated by this wood. I will be very thankful if you allow me to spend a day here so I can admire the beauty of this place before dying."

The bandit laughed and said, "Don't think you can fool me so easily; I will not change my decision in a day. I have never spared a single traveler in my whole life. Don't even think about running away, as you can't escape from my dogs."

After spending a few hours with the bandit, the wise man asked him how he ended up in the forest. The bandit replied, "When I was a young boy, I was stupid and terrible at everything; I failed in almost every aspect of life. People didn't like me as I looked ugly because of my big face. On top of this, my father was abusive and would beat me often. Overall, I was a big failure. One day, frustrated with my life, I ran away from my family to live a harsh life in the forest. I became a bandit looting people; I feel better living away from all of them."

Before the execution the next day, the bandit asked, "You have spent a day with me, but I still don't feel kind to you. If you can tell me why, I can consider sparing your life."

The wise man thought for a while and replied, "The reason for this is that you are harsh and cruel to yourself. I often notice you blaming yourself for all the failures and the bad things which happened in your life. Unless you are kind to yourself, you can't feel kindness for others."

Instead of getting offended, the bandit was delighted with his answer. He allowed him to go with all his valuables. Sometime later, he also decided to leave the jungle and the life of a bandit.

Do you remember a time when, like the bandit, you have told yourself, "I am stupid", or "I can't do this right", or "I am a big failure", or "I am not good enough"? Now ask yourself whether you would be comfortable looking in the eyes of a close friend and saying these same words to them. I'm guessing the answer is 'No'. We would never beat up a friend over the mistakes they made years ago. We would never expect a friend to push themselves when they are exhausted and need rest. Then why are we so often unkind and hard on ourselves? Why do we find it difficult to treat ourselves with the same love and respect we want to show others?

Don't you agree that we need to be nicer to someone who is always there for us and sharing our pain? Then why are we not nice to ourselves, our solo companion for life? Often in the race to achieve our goals, we become so "busy" that we hardly get the time to remember and acknowledge this best companion. This is one of the reasons why we often forget all etiquette while dealing with ourselves. We often hold ourselves to higher standards and whip ourselves for past mistakes, ignoring our past successes and small achievements. The effect of this behavior is that slowly, we start disliking ourselves. All the negative self-talk and self-criticism gradually results in low self-esteem, low confidence, and unhappiness. Moreover, this self-harming behavior is one of the most frequent causes of depression and anxiety in today's world.

Think for a while and check if you have a habit of setting high goals for yourself, and whether you see yourself as not good enough when you can't meet them? You are not alone; it has become a norm nowadays to keep raising the bar as we constantly compare ourselves to those around us. There is nothing wrong with having goals and aiming hard for them, but they need to be realistic and achievable. Moreover, we should not fall prey to harsh inner critics if we fail to achieve these goals. The real problem starts when we focus only on our weaknesses and perceived flaws and blame ourselves for everything during this criticism. While there are many mountains to climb, permit yourself to do it at a pace that is in harmony with yourself.

Now, spare a minute and check if you are overly critical of your failures or mistakes. Though it is essential that we examine our flaws regularly, we should not mistake this exercise for self-punishment. Before self-criticizing, we need to ask ourselves, "What am I gaining from this exercise?" Always remember, a true friend is a better guide than a harsh critic when you need to change.

Most people believe that a person's true nature is revealed by how kindly they speak with strangers. Yet, the truth is that their true character is revealed by how kindly they talk to themselves. The early Stoic Cleanthes once overheard another philosopher speaking unkindly to himself when he thought no one was listening. Cleanthes stopped and reminded him, "You aren't talking to a bad man."

According to Dr. Kristen Neff, we are harsh or sometimes even cruel in how we address ourselves because it is all happening inside our heads. So, the next time you find yourself with harsh self-talk going inside your mind, think for a while: is it necessary to be right rather than kind? Then try to pause to restate the point in a softer tone of voice. Starting a conversation in a softer tone will help you build a friendship with yourself. You will soon realize that this new communication method will help develop a compassionate inner voice that can change the overall experience of self-talks.

Forgive Yourself, and Then Let It Go

Once, there was a cruel person called Angulimala, famous for killing innocent people. He would cut the fingers of the people he killed and wear them on a necklace. After he met Buddha, he was utterly changed. He threw away his necklace and weapons and followed Buddha to become a monk.

One day, Buddha asked him to go out as a monk to collect alms. He was reluctant to go out and face people but could not refuse Buddha. Once he went to the village, people recognized him and started throwing stones at him. Injured and disappointed, he returned to Buddha and cried, "People are never going to forgive me for my gruesome acts!"

Buddha smiled and said, "It hardly matters if they forgive you or not. First, you should forgive yourself."

Later, when people came to know about Angulimala's transformation, they came to Buddha and asked, "Can he have a peaceful and balanced mind after all that he has done?"

The Buddha answered, "Yes. He had badly harmed himself, resulting in all this violence. Now, he has forgiven himself and is thus slowly trying to attain a peaceful mind."

Do you think there is sense in repeatedly punishing ourselves for our past mistakes? Regrets are a way of punishing ourselves for something we can no longer change. The first thing we need to accept is that nobody is perfect in life. Isn't this a good enough reason to be gentle with ourselves when confronted with our own shortcomings? It is important to keep reminding ourselves of all the good decisions we have made and the lives we have touched. Our family and friends value us not because we are faultless but because of who we are. If you know this, don't you think it's better to talk to yourself with love and support during difficult times rather than blaming yourself all the time? We should take our time and think for a while: Are our regrets really so inexcusable that we cannot forgive ourselves? When Angulimala can do it, why can't we?

Though forgiving ourselves is necessary to move forward, self-forgiveness should not be taken as a means of excusing ourselves or ignoring our wrongdoings. Self-forgiveness is also not about going without being punished; neither is it a sign of weakness. It means accepting what has happened and moving on with our life without mulling over past situations that cannot be changed. It also means showing compassion for ourselves and recognizing our humanity. Remember, we all mess up; therefore, forgiving yourself is the first step if you want to move on.

Have you noticed that in real life, when we make a mistake, we are punished only once. Still, we repetitively punish ourselves for the mistakes of the past. Don't you think, like others, we need to have empathy for ourselves? Punishing ourselves is easy, but self-empathy requires greater self-awareness, discipline, and a commitment to finding helpful solutions. Self-empathy is also an acknowledgment that we deserve compassion like all human beings. It is also about acknowledging that, as humans, we are fallible, and mistakes are part of the broad human experience.

After twenty-seven years, when Nelson Mandela walked out of the brutal Robben Island prison, he said, "As I walked out the door towards the gate that would lead to my freedom, I knew if I didn't leave my bitterness and hatred behind, I'd still be in prison." Like Mandela, sometimes it is necessary to practice forgiveness for ourselves; otherwise, we will remain in our own prison, repetitively punishing ourselves. It is also crucial to let go of shame, blame, and bitterness by recognizing that we are doing the best with what we currently have. We need to remember that the only person we can control is ourselves. With this firm belief, we have the power to escape from the internal despair and depression caused by any past mistakes.

Forgiving ourselves is not a one-off process but something we need to practice daily. It can be as simple as saying, "I forgive myself" each morning as part of a ritual. There is an ancient practice on the Polynesian island of the south pacific, Ho'oponopono, for reconciliation and self-forgiveness.

The simple prayer goes like this:

"I'm sorry,

Please forgive me,

Thank you,

I love you."

To "cleanse" yourself of bad feelings and heal yourself, chant the above mantra repeatedly while sitting with your eyes closed as a kind of meditation each morning as part of your ritual. Reciting these four simple phrases with regular practice will help you find peace in yourself and develop self-love and self-esteem when you need it most.

Respect Yourself and Your Dreams

Once, a new principal joined a school. He thought of introducing himself to the students by going to each class. He went from class to class to interact with the students.

First, he went to the kindergarten students and asked, "How many of you want to share your dreams with me?" All the students raised their hands. A few said that they wanted to be president of the country. A few were interested in becoming astronauts, a few pilots, a few sportsmen, and the last few said they wanted to be movie stars. The principal was delighted to hear this. This same pattern followed in younger grades.

But he saw a strange change when he asked the same question in higher-level classes. He realized that the number of hands raised was getting smaller and smaller. When he prompted others, they said they were unsure about their dreams. Finally, nobody raised their hands when he asked the same question in the high school classes.

When we are small, we all have big dreams and a strong belief that we have all the power to achieve them. As we grow up and start engaging in negative self-talk, we start feeling we are no longer capable of achieving these dreams. We are so scared of our inner critic that we slowly stop taking risks and often downplay our goals by labeling them silly fantasies. Later, when this critic has taken over our minds, we even stop dreaming and feel unworthy. Therefore, it is necessary to watch for our negative self-talk and interrupt the inner voice when it says that we are unqualified to achieve our goals. Take a deep breath and think, instead of being our worst critics, why can't we support ourselves like a best friend to achieve our goals? Then try to replace the negative self-talk with a piece of positive advice you may give to a good friend who is anxious about their own goals.

Do you know that if you act like a good friend to yourself, you will be more willing to take risks to achieve your dreams? Why? Because you will be aware that your inner self will not attack you in a merciless way if you fail. Never let someone crush your dreams, not even yourself.

As singers John and Edward say in their song from the album *Voice of a Rebel*:

"Respect your dreams
Go live your life
Don't write yourself off
Put up a fight,
Protect your heart
From those who hate
Respect your dreams
It's not too late."

Alan Cohen writes in his book, *The Tao Made Easy*, "To say or imply 'I am unworthy' is not a statement of humility. It is an assertion of arrogance as you deny that we are here for a purpose and must do our part to manifest our destiny. Do not fall into the trap of believing you are unqualified and do not deserve to achieve meaningful results or have good things for yourself. Such self-negation is a denial of your identity and calling." Later in the book, Alan tells a story in which a respected teacher, Chou Huo, has committed suicide. When Lao Tzu is asked the reason for his death, he replies, "He has amassed a great deal of information, but he did not know how to live. The tragic death of a man the world honored but who could not honor himself." Even Confucius stressed on the importance of self-respect when he said, "Human beings are worthy of respect, but people should respect themselves first."

Love Yourself and Be Your Own Best Friend

Throughout his life, Roman philosopher Seneca wrote letters to his friend Lucilius, an official in Sicily, advising him on becoming a better Stoic philosopher.

In one of the letters, Seneca wrote how he is learning to be kind to himself. He wrote that, as a very old man, he was working to be kinder to himself and trying to make sure that he also loves himself like a good friend. Seneca emphasizes the importance of being your own friend by saying that the person who befriends themself will never be alone and will be a friend of all.

As he wrote, "I have learned to be a friend to myself, great improvement this indeed, such a one can never be alone. The one who is a friend to himself is a friend to all humanity."

Don't you want to love yourself as a good friend like Seneca? Self-love is a matter of self-acceptance without fulfilling a specific condition or living up to some particular standards. No one can teach you how to love yourself; it has to come from within. Like all relationships, self-love requires patience and kindness to flourish. It will not happen overnight, but slowly, your inner-self will respond to the love and care you put into it. As philosopher Plutarch said, "The best thing you can do for yourself is to get to know yourself, your true wisdom, and accept and love who you truly are—the good, the bad, and the ugly. What we achieve inwardly will change outer reality."

One of the essential lessons to learn early in life is to love and accept ourselves unconditionally. We all have strengths and weaknesses; sometimes we succeed, sometimes we fail, sometimes we are correct, and sometimes we are wrong. We should allow ourselves to be who we are. Don't we accept our friends as they are? So why do we find it difficult to accept ourselves as we are? Don't you think it is worth having an affirmation every day saying, "Today, I will befriend the person I already am"? This affirmation will remind us that our friendship with ourselves is without any selfishness.

Mirza Ghalib was a highly renowned poet of the eighteenth century in India. One day, he was listening to the poems of another poet, Momin Khan. He was so impressed with one of the verses that he announced he was ready to give up all his poems in exchange for this. The translation of that verse was, "You are with me in those times when there is no one else standing beside me."

The meaning in these lines is so touching and can remind us of the deep loneliness we feel during hard times when everyone deserts us. Then suddenly, we will realize that our "self" is still standing at our side despite all odds. So, the next time you find yourself in a difficult situation alone and cannot think of what to do, just put your hand on your heart and wish yourself well for the support.

Take Good Care of Yourself

Growing up, I frequently visited one of my uncles, whom we nicknamed 'Machine Uncle' due to his great interest in machines. He had excellent knowledge of all the devices in his home. He would often talk about the importance of taking good care of and frequently servicing these machines so they can run smoothly for a long time. We often saw him servicing his bike, fans, or appliances in the kitchen.

Unfortunately, he missed caring for the most crucial machine, his own body. He spent long hours working without taking much care of himself. All this resulted in the difficult last years of his life. Later, he regretted not taking better care of himself during his earlier years.

In one of our last meetings, he told me, "When I was not kind to my body, how can I expect my body to be kind to me."

While traveling in a plane, have you listened carefully to the pre-flight safety instructions? In one of them, the flight attendants tell us, "In the unlikely event of a sudden loss in cabin pressure, oxygen masks will drop down from the panel above your head. Secure your own mask before helping others." Many of you may question whether this advice is reasonable. We always like to help our loved ones first, especially our children. The rationale behind this advice is that you will fumble around trying to help others and maybe pass out yourself if you don't have enough oxygen. There are more chances that you would be able to help others better once you have secured your mask.

This is an important analogy for people who always run around taking care of everything and everyone before themselves. They try to act like a superhero, always putting everyone else's needs before theirs. However, they fail to acknowledge that they are not giving proper attention to themselves in this process. It would help if they noticed that most superheroes in movies live everyday lives and only act as heroes for a short time when needed. So, it's better to accept our limitations as humans and good to say 'no' rather than loading more and more onto our shoulders. If we accept every new request life throws at us, we will soon burn out. Therefore, if we want to take care of our loved ones, we must adequately prioritize our self-care first. As philosopher Ralph Waldo explains, "It is one of the most beautiful compensations of life that no man can sincerely try to help others without helping himself first."

I am confident that you will agree that one of the best ways to show kindness to yourself is by taking good care of yourself. You don't have to plan big things but rather try to do little things that make you calm and happy. Start making routines for self-care, giving yourself "me time" each day to carve out something that brings you joy. You can write, read, play a musical instrument, prepare a pleasant meal for yourself, or do anything else that you love to do without rushing out. Try to cook and eat healthy meals, exercise, go for a walk, get enough sleep, and self-groom. All of these little things will help you release stress and let you feel good about yourself. Sometimes this routine can include just going over your thoughts and childhood memories or spending time with the people who make you happy. As we show our love in relationships through random acts of appreciation and consideration, we need to show love to ourselves through small acts of kindness.

Compliment Yourself

Once, I was having dinner with one of my friends in the hospitality business. I casually asked him about the challenges faced in his business.

He replied, "In our industry, we try to take the best care of our customers. We do everything to make our customers happy, but people seldom remember the excellent service. On the other hand, if there is a small mistake, they try to make a big fuss about that." He added, "How good would it be if people complimented our good services in the same way they criticize our mistakes."

We all love to compliment others, but we are too stingy in giving compliments to ourselves. While it is necessary to acknowledge the achievements of others, it is also important not to ignore your own.

Giving yourself compliments is as beneficial as receiving them from others. It makes you feel good about yourself and reminds you of how awesome you are. Once you know your awesomeness, you shrug off all negative emotions holding you back and start believing in yourself.

Try to remember a time when you complimented yourself for something you were proud of or a small win. If not, next time during such a moment, stop for a minute, congratulate yourself, and live on it. When you praise yourself and relish the achievement by patting your back, you will notice the compliment's fantastic effect on your morale and self-esteem.

Accept Yourself

During my first visit to the gym, I was surprised to see the wall full of mirrors. Later, when I became friendly with one of the trainers, I asked him why they had so many mirrors in the gym.

The trainer smiled and said, "Most people think these mirrors are just for observing their alignment and posture while exercising and to help improve that. But over time, I have observed a different perspective. Many people who are not in shape try to avoid the mirrors as they feel they are looking at an unacceptable person. When they come to the gym and see themselves in the mirrors for an extended period, they feel comfortable and start accepting themselves. These mirrors, in turn, help people get comfortable in their own skin."

Have you observed that even in a perfect garden, if you look close enough, you will see some weeds here or there? However, that is something you need to ignore while enjoying the beauty of that place. The same applies when we look inwards at the beauty of our heart, the garden of our inner space. To enjoy our inner garden, we must learn to focus on our perfections and ignore our imperfections. Self-acceptance is the first step of one's journey of growth. Accepting our flaws makes us look more natural and beautiful from the inside and outside. According to famous American psychologist Abraham Maslow, acceptance, especially in the areas where you feel helpless or weak, is a vital step towards becoming emotionally mature and realizing your potential.

17th-century Japanese poet Matsuo Basho wrote a beautiful poem, "My horse clip-clopping over a field ... oh ho! I'm part of the picture!!" This poem teaches us a good lesson: once we see ourselves as an essential part of life's great picture, we can realize our importance in life and thus start loving and accepting ourselves. It also teaches that, like others, we are an integral part of the picture. It is an important life lesson that we must remember: We can't progress forward unless we completely accept ourselves.

Conclusion

In her bestselling book, *Eat, Pray, Love,* Elizabeth Gilbert writes that she walked into a building in New York City in a hurry one day. She was rushing towards the elevator when she caught a glimpse of herself in a mirror. However, unable to recognize herself, she thought, "Oh, look! I know her. She's my friend."

Gilbert moved toward her reflection with a smile, ready to hug this person, when she realized she was looking at herself. Later, when she was in Rome, she felt sad and alone, but then she remembered this incident. Thinking of that day in New York brought her some comfort. She was journaling, and she wrote the following at the bottom of the page:

"Never forget that once upon a time, in an unguarded moment, you recognized yourself as a friend."

As Buddha said, "You can search throughout the entire universe for someone more deserving of your love and affection than you are yourself, and that person is not to be found anywhere. You deserve your love and affection as much as anybody in the entire universe."

"To love oneself," wrote Oscar Wilde, "is the beginning of a life-long romance." As is the tale of every love story, time will bring both sun and storm, testing our deepest intentions on how we relate to ourselves. So, the tale goes on, and there will be good and bad days that will test our relationship with ourselves. On the good days, love comes easy as our self-esteem stands tall on our accomplishments. In contrast, on the bad days, as we only remember our faults, our self-esteem feels low. We start blaming ourselves for our failures and try to abandon ourselves. One way to win back our hearts and reclaim our well-being is through self-compassion. Self-compassion is something we always have in our power to do whatever bad happens in our lives. **When you love yourself enough, you will find the whole world looks like a beautiful place.**

While writing this book, I remembered many times I bullied myself for past mistakes instead of treating myself as a friend. At times, I was even cruel in pushing myself too hard, just trying to impress others. I stopped writing and took time to reflect on my inner thoughts. Then, with a heavy sense of remorse, I wrote an apology letter to myself. Now, I keep that letter near me to remind me to be kind to myself. It is a start of a journey of friendship and love with myself.

There is a line in the song from the album *Living Mirage* by The Head and The Heart,

"Until you learn to love yourself
The door is locked to someone else."

So, if you are waiting for someone to love you, first start loving yourself. Be gentle to yourself and try to become your own friend. Appreciate all the progress you've made so far and tell yourself, "Great job!" with a big smile.

Keys for Being Kind to Yourself

- Remember, the most important person to keep forgiving is yourself.
- Start your day by greeting yourself in the morning as you would greet a good friend. Then take time to remind yourself of all your good qualities.
- Speak to yourself as you would speak to a small child; use your name, not "I," when talking to yourself.
- Praise and compliment yourself when you do something incredible; every micro-win and even a small act of kindness needs a big applause.
- Kiss your hands occasionally, and say to yourself, "You're awesome!" (I do that every morning and every now and then.)
- Be compassionate with yourself when things go wrong; always remember that nobody is perfect.
- Try your best to avoid stress as it is another way to torture yourself.
- Make your bed, keep your room clean, clean your desk; all these things are part of loving oneself.
- Take breaks, share your problems with friends, and learn to say no.
- Meditation is an excellent way to reset the mind, like resetting the phone when things don't work.
- Remember to smile. It is one of the best ways to be kind to yourself.

Commandment IV

Thou Shall Guard Your Tongue

Those who guard their tongues
keep themselves away from misfortunes.
— Bible Proverbs 21:23

Once, an old weaver from a remote village went to the city to meet his friend working in a large garment factory. After meeting his friend, he asked him if he could see how they do modern weaving in the city.

His friend took him on a tour of the factory. After they had toured the factory, he took the old weaver to a strange big machine with long wires running from its sides.

"I am fully familiar with all the other machines, but I have never seen a big machine like this in my whole life," said the surprised old weaver. "But what is this machine for?"

"My friend, this machine is run by electricity," his friend smiled and replied.

"It can weave in minutes what other machines do in a day. But you must be extremely careful while operating this machine. If you make even a small mistake, it can ruin more material in a minute than all the other machines use in a day."

Can you see how our tongues could be like this electric-powered machine? If used properly, it has the power to weave a beautiful life for us. However, if misused, it can also be the reason for our downfall. We can use our tongues to say good words, which create and build strong relationships while also bringing tremendous happiness to others. On the other hand, using bad words can discourage others and destroy and tear down relationships. Depending on its use, it can provide us with the quickest opportunity for success or downfall. As the mast of the boat can steer and set the direction even amid strong winds, in the same way if we steer our tongue correctly, we have the power to take our life in a positive direction. Sometimes we may feel that the results of our words are not imminent, but they are like seeds that each of us continue to sow into our lives. If the seeds are good, it is sure the crop we harvest will also be good.

Imagine waking up one morning and seeing two magic keys by the side of your bed with an explanatory note that one of them can open the door to prosperity and bliss. At the same time, the other brings misery and enmity. I am sure you will agree that the choice will be easy. Yet many people say they are faced with a similar choice every day, and too often, they choose wrongly and regret it later. Instead of using the right power of our tongue to create peace, blessing, and love, which can open the door for prosperity, we misuse it and create strife, cursing, and hatred, opening the door for misery. Every single day we have a choice to make between these two. We can either speak words that produce life and health or fear and death. Therefore, if you want to control your life, control your choice of words.

Words Once Spoken Can Never Be Recalled

In her novel 'Ceremony', Leslie Marmon Silko recounts the story of a witch competition. All the witches competed to see who could devise the scariest thing. A few of the witches impressed everyone with magic potions. Then came the witches who jumped in and out of animal skins. Then a few thought up charms and spells.

Finally, there was only one remaining. She said, "I don't have any charms or powers to show, but I have a story. As I tell the story, it will begin to happen."

At first, everyone laughed, but later she was allowed to tell her story. The story was full of awful things, fear and slaughter, disease, and blood. All the witches were frightened to death by listening to the story.

When she completed her story, the other witches said, "Okay, you win; you take the prize, but we can't get along with what you said just now. Take it back. Call that story back."

But the witch just shook her head and said, "You can call all your charms and spells back, but the words once loose can't be called back."

Did you notice that in this story, the words of the witch proved more potent than any potions, transformation, charm, or spell: they actually made things happen, and there was no way to undo them. According to an ancient saying, three things can never be taken back: a shot arrow, a spoken word, and a lost opportunity. Words are powerful and magical like arrows; once released, they cannot be recalled, the harm they do cannot be stopped, and they cannot always be predicted. Therefore, we must take extreme care when using our words, so they don't go astray like arrows.

Have you heard the saying that a great forest can be set on fire by a tiny spark? In the same way, the words from our mouths can put the course of one's life on fire. We should always be aware of the power of our speech and remember that the harm done by it can never be reversed. There is an old saying: "If you have taken a wrong path, you can turn around, but harsh words can never be taken back." This is the reason Spanish writer Miguel de Cervantes advised in his book *Don Quixote*, "Think twice before you speak."

Confucius was of this notion that our words should always follow our deeds. That is why he said, "Words once spoken are as hard to put back as water spilled from a jug, so a wise person always gets the things done first, then talks about them. Never let your words go further than your actions."

The Damage Done by Lies Can't Be Undone

A man started telling malicious lies about a neighbor in the community. Later, he realized his mistake and began to feel remorse. He went to a sage and begged for forgiveness, saying he would do anything to make amends.

The sage told the man, "Take this bag of grains which has a small hole. Carry this bag on your back till it is empty and return to me tomorrow."

The man thought this was a strange request, but it was a simple task, and he did it gladly. The next day when he returned to tell the sage that he had done it, the sage said, "Now, go and gather all the grains back in this new bag."

The man tried but came back with an empty bag. He told the sage, "I cannot find any grains; the animals and insects ate them all."

The sage replied, "Like you are not able to recollect the grains, once your words are loose, you cannot make amends for the damage they have done."

A while ago, I was at a children's birthday party where the kids were playing the game 'Chinese Whispers'. In this game, the first person starts by whispering a statement in the ear of the next person. The person who heard the whisper passes the message to the next person. None of them are allowed to repeat themselves. When the message gets back to the person who started, he has to speak it aloud, so everyone knows the difference between the original and final statements. It is so funny to see that, in most cases, the meaning of the statement is completely distorted once it has passed many ears.

Sometimes, similar to the game, when malicious lies reach different ears, the meaning becomes more and more distorted. If we know that gossiping can cause such harm, shouldn't we be more cautious about the words we speak? Especially when it is about someone who is not there to defend themselves. So, the next time, before you say something bad about a person, ask yourself, "How would I feel if someone said this about me?"

In *Analects*, Confucius mentions that fools spend all their time in malicious gossip and spreading lies. In contrast, the wise person spends that time paying attention to their inner heart, learning new things, and imparting this knowledge to others.

Consider Whether It Is Worth Listening

Once a wise man was visited by an acquaintance. Eager to share some juicy gossip, the man asked if he would like to know a story he had just heard about a friend of his.

"Hold on a minute," The wise man replied. "Before telling me anything, let me know, is it something good about him?"

The acquaintance said, "No, on the contrary...."

The wise man lifted his hand to stop the man from speaking. "So, you are certain that what you want to say is nothing good about my friend. But tell me, is that useful or necessary to me?"

A little defeated, the man answered, "No, not really."

The wise man said, "Then please don't say anything at all."

> The man reacted, eager to share the gossip, "You should listen to it; I think it is true!"
>
> The wise man answered, "The truth will only matter if what you want to say is either good about my friend or necessary for me."

We all know that derogatory or damaging talks are bad, and we mostly try to restrain ourselves. However, we still see no harm in listening to these talks. Do you know that in the long term, gossip can create negative vibes and generate hostility between people? Then the person who listens to these conversations becomes worse than the person who tells them because negative talks cannot do any harm if no one is listening. Listening to these talks can act like adding fuel to the fire. In turn, it also encourages the person who is spreading these rumors.

Like the wise man, always ask yourself before listening to a topic: Is it good? Is it useful? If it passes these filters, only then be ready to attend the gossipmongers. If not, either find a tactful way to make it pass or, worst case, keep it to yourself. Whatever we do, idle minds will always come up with tales to defame others, and there is no stopping them. But as a responsible person, we have to decide, 'The buck stops with me.' Once we start ignoring these gossips, it will automatically stop spreading.

Three Precious Gems

> Once a king who was getting married asked his minister about the secret of a successful marriage. The minister smiled and replied, "Your majesty, I think I am not the right person to answer this as I have frequent fights with my wife. But I know

a poor farmer in our village known for his successful marriage. The couple always looks happy, and nobody has ever seen a fight between them. "

The king immediately summoned the poor farmer and asked him about the secret of his marriage.

The farmer humbly replied, "Though I have a very small farm, it is sufficient to meet my family's needs. However, the success of my marriage is the three precious gems we gift each other. Sometimes many times in a day. These gems are the pillar of our marriage."

In a surprise, the king asked, "What are these three precious gems, and from where did you get these? "

The farmer smiled and replied, "The first precious gem is the 'harmonious or sweet words' we share often. When I want to encourage her, I give her a gift of these sweet words, the same way she uses the sweet words to encourage me from time to time. When she is talking, I listen to her with full attention. Listening is the second precious gem."

The curious king asked, "And what is the third one?"

The farmer answered, "Whenever she gets angry, I always use silence to calm her down. She also follows the same whenever I am frustrated. This is the third gem. These are the only three precious gems which are enough to make everyone feel special and happy."

Remember, nothing in this world is as sweet as sweet words; therefore, like the farmer, always share this first precious gem with your partner. Sweet words strengthen the relationship; in contrast,

71

harsh words slowly deteriorate the relationships over time. Always remember our words have the power to either enhance our relationships or destroy it. Therefore, we need to choose them wisely. Every person in this world needs love, support, and encouragement, even when they don't seem to be fulfilling the expectations others have for them.

When we encourage our partners with our harmonious words, we feed them with the necessary food they need to build a healthier self-esteem. Sometimes we may use harsh words for our loved ones with good intentions, but these good intentions become useless when coated with negative words. Physicians add sugar to bitter medicines so that patients can take them easily. In the same way, while giving harsh advice, we need to mix it with sweet words so that they may be received better.

To keep our relationship strong, we must also develop our listening skills, the second precious gem from the story. In her famous TED talk, Evy Poumpouras said, "Make people feel special. Listen to people. Be present. Nobody matters more than that person across from you." She later stressed that when we listen, we should speak less. She reminded the audience of a myth that we all carry: if we talk more, we can control the conversation. But the truth is the exact opposite: the person who speaks less is in control because we're giving it all up; we're an open book. The part of the talk I liked was the suggestion about using the Pareto principle of the 80:20 rule in everyday communication. We should be listening 80% of the time, and the rest 20% of the time should be used for speaking. This rule is especially significant when it's something that we desire and need to learn because if we're only talking, we're not actually learning anything.

Publilius Syrus, the Latin writer of the first century B.C., once said, "I often regret that I have spoken but never my silence." The third precious gem, 'silence,' is one of the panaceas for all problems. Most of the time, anger and frustration subside with themselves if the other person is using silence as their defense. Silence should never be considered a sign of weakness, but actually, it is a sign of strength. Have you ever noticed that not everyone can keep calm and silent during a difficult situation? We often argue to prove who is right or wrong. In the short term, we may win an argument, but sooner or later, we might discover that we have not really convinced the other person. We have only worn them out, and throughout the process, we may have lost a friend.

It's Better to Be Silent in front of Foolish People

There was a large tree on the banks of a river where certain birds had built their nests. One day, the sky was overcast with thick dark clouds, and rain fell in vast streams.

The birds residing in the nests saw a troop of monkeys at the foot of the tree. The monkeys were wet and shivering with cold. One of the birds called out to them, "Monkeys! Why don't you build a house that can protect you from the rain?" The monkeys, not ready to take any advice, ignored the bird. But the bird kept on saying, "See? We build ourselves nests with straw collected using nothing but our beaks. You all are blessed with hands and feet, and yet you are suffering?"

The monkeys took this as criticism and became exceedingly irritated. They said amongst themselves, "Those birds there, sitting comfortably in their warm nests, are laughing at us! Let them do so till the rain lasts."

As soon as the rain had subsided, the troop of monkeys mounted the tree and tore all the nests to pieces. The birds flew for their lives while their eggs fell to the ground and broke.

Do you remember a time when like the birds, you have given a piece of advice to someone, but the recipient, instead of thanking you, got irritated, and your advice was completely ignored? You are not alone; it happens with all of us. We try to advise others with good intentions, but some people are never ready to listen. Therefore, never advise people until they ask for it. A wise person is always ready to ask for advice, but an ignorant one will never. We also need to understand that people don't need advice when they are stressed; they need empathy and someone who can listen to them.

Confucius said that though we should advise people to the best of our ability and guide them properly, when they snub us or there is no hope of success, we should stop. We should not keep on advising without watching other people's expressions. Extra carefulness should be taken when guarding our tongues in front of fools, as they will spit our good advice like a bitter dose of medicine on our face. Be careful to understand the person we are talking to, and accordingly look to see what words can be said and what is better left unsaid. Wise men are not always silent, but they know when to be. Therefore, it's important to learn when to speak and when to hold your tongue.

How to Guard Our Tongues

"Who left the garden gate open?" shouted the father as he entered his cottage. "Those blasted goats have been at the vegetables again. How many times do I have to warn you to keep the gate closed?" His frightened family promised to follow this rule in the future, and for a few days, everything went well. But one day, one of the children, in a hurry to join his friends, forgot to shut the gate. Some neighborhood goats entered the garden and ate all the vegetables.

When the father returned home and saw what had happened, he became furious. "That's the last straw. We need vegetables from our garden to have enough food to eat. I see that I can't rely on my family to keep the garden gate shut, so I am going to wall up the gate opening so that those goats will never get in again to destroy my garden."

"But Father," asked one of his children, "How will we get in and out of the house if there is no gate?"

"I am sorry," was the reply, "But we will just have to climb over the wall each time."

"But won't it look ridiculous climbing over a wall every time you enter or leave home?"

"It's better to look a little ridiculous," replied the father, "than to go hungry."

Like the gate in the story, our lips are the gates to our tongue. So, whenever there is temptation to speak evil gossip or make fun of somebody, we need to seal our lips like the gates. Humans can tame wild animals, birds, reptiles, and sea creatures, but we still find it extremely difficult to tame our own wild tongues.

Suppose you feel like you often surrender to the temptation of speaking and misusing your power of speech. In that case, you should try some periodical exercises in silence. The great Persian poet Rumi once said, "Silence is the language of God, all else is poor translation." Therefore, at regular intervals, have 'Tongue Fasting' or 'Silent time,' where you observe silence for at least some time every day.

During this extended period of verbal abstinence, keep reminding yourself of the Chinese folk saying, 'Trouble comes from the mouth.' This exercise will help you have more control over your tongue. Over time you will be more sensible about your speech, and guarding your tongue will become more manageable. The art of knowing when to speak and when to hold your tongue is a life-long learning process that requires a lot of self-discipline.

Train Your Tongue to Speak Good Things

A sage selected one of his students to start giving discourses in his absence. The rest of the students were upset with this decision as they were not given this chance. The sage was able to see this discontentment in his students and thought to resolve it.

One day he asked the students to join him for a walk on the path toward the village. On the way, they passed by the corpse of a dead animal. One of them said: "How rotten this animal has become!" The other exclaimed, "How it is deformed!" A third cried out, "What a stink!!"

After everyone had said something terrible about the corpse, the sage asked the student he had selected, "You haven't said anything about the dead animal. Have you not noticed anything in the corpse?"

The student replied, "Sir, I haven't noticed anything the others mentioned, but I noticed its tail! The beast has a beautiful small tail!"

The sage replied to others, "Now you understand why I have selected him to give the discourses. He spoke only good things about the animal ignoring his defects. To be a good speaker, you need to train your tongue to speak good things while overlooking the bad things."

At a high level, we commonly use three different types of speech in our communication, positive, neutral, and negative. When we say good things about others, it becomes a part of our positive speech. On the other hand, when we are telling facts objectively or providing constructive feedback, it becomes an example of neutral speech. However, when we criticize others, it becomes part of negative talk. After we have trained our tongue using a period of silence, we can try to start tasting the words before speaking as we taste the food before serving. Unless you feel your words are either neutral or positive, never say them; let silence be your good for the most part.

When you open your mouth, say only what is necessary, and use kind words which can heal others rather than create lifelong wounds. Sometimes, instead of heroic and blunt truth-telling, we need to massage the truth, so it becomes loving and gentle. There are many attributes in every person, good and bad. It is the characteristic of a wise person to highlight the good qualities while overlooking the bad ones.

When I was growing up, I remember my grandmother reminded us that if we criticize others, especially behind their back, our good karmas will depreciate. I don't know if it is true; however, as she also practiced the same, people in my family still remember her as a nice lady. Confucius once said, "Not having made myself perfect, I have no time to criticize others." Don't you think instead of wasting our precious time criticizing others, we need to spend that time working on making ourselves better?

Words Can Create A New World for Others

One day a learned man visiting a village blessed a small boy and said, "I am sure you will grow up as a wise person."

A passerby mocked the learned man and asked how he knew that the boy would become a wise person.

The learned man replied to the passerby, "I know you will soon become a fool who will boast about his ego."

The angry passerby immediately started shouting at him, offended by his harsh words.

The learned man smiled and spoke, "See how soon you started behaving the way I have said. You have proved that words can come true with your behavior."

We know that words are sacred and have the power to come true, so we should use them with care and try to practice positive speech. For the same reason, shouldn't we think a dozen times before saying something demoralizing to ourselves and the people around us, especially those we love? When our words reflect fairness, love, and kindness, we automatically uplift those around us and create a peaceful and kinder environment. When we encourage and advise, we make good use of our speech and rise above the challenges, bringing light into our lives and the lives we touch. Once you start choosing your words wisely, you will notice a positive difference in yourself as well as the people around you.

The Indian mystic poet, Kabir Das, crystallizes the power of spoken words in one of his poems. He teaches us that when we use positive speech, it creates a sense of joy for the listener and creates harmonious and composed vibes. So, the next time your kids come up to validate if their new dreams will come true, instead of saying, "I hope so," say, "I am sure it will." Or when someone asks you how you are doing, say "Excellent" or "Great," and you will feel the same.

Conclusion

In his book, *The Biology of Belief*, American biologist Bruce Lipton narrates a practice followed by the tribes of the Solomon Islands. When the tribals want to cut down a tree, they don't use an axe; they just surround it and curse it for hours every day. Apparently, within a few weeks, the tree dries up and dies.

Unintentionally are you doing the same while using harsh words to your children, convincing yourself that it is discipline rather than anger? Or to your spouse, thinking that it is their fault rather than your venting? Or to your parents, to justify that you know more than them? Or to your subordinates thinking it is their bad performance rather than your hurt ego? Remember, these harsh words have negative effects. With these words, we instill beliefs in the listeners' minds that will continue harming them forever.

In his masterpiece book *The Alchemist*, Paulo Coelho narrates the mystical story of a shepherd boy Santiago. He yearns to travel to the Egyptian pyramids, searching for a treasure. In his quest to find the treasure, he meets an alchemist in the middle of an African desert. When the alchemist offers him a delicious wine, he asks, "Isn't wine prohibited here?"

"It's not what enters the men's mouth that's evil," said the alchemist, **"It's what comes out of their mouths, that is."**

Knowing this, we must be responsible for what comes from our mouths. Our words are like seeds; kind words sow the seeds of a plant bearing beautiful flowers, but cruel words can sow the seeds of poison ivy, which hurt those around it. Therefore, we need to be very careful and responsible for the messages we send to those around us. We are all influencers in our own ways. And we should feel responsible for ensuring that we positively and constructively influence everyone around us to make this world a better place.

Keys for Guarding Your Tongue

➤ **THINK** before you speak. Is it Thoughtful, Helpful, Inspiring, Necessary, and Kind?

➤ The first logical step is to commit, be it 15 minutes a day, to being conscious of your words; consider it a period of positive reinforcement.

➤ It's better to keep silent, especially when influenced by a negative passion such as anger, greed, or jealousy.

➤ Remember that winning the argument is not always necessary at the cost of deteriorating the relationship.

➤ Once you know that your words were offensive, rude, or have hurt someone, acknowledge it, admit it and apologize as soon as possible.

Commandment V

Thou Shall Not Dwell on the Past

Forget the former things.
Do not dwell on the past.
See, I am doing a new thing!
Now it springs up; do you not perceive it?
I am making a way in the wilderness
& Streams in the wasteland. (Isaiah 43:18:19)

A soldier was taking care of his mother during her final stages of a terminal illness when suddenly, he got a call from his unit to report to the border post. He was unwilling, but his mother forced him to respond to his call of duty. He kept thinking about her at his border post and grew exceedingly sorrowful. Every day, he wrote a letter to his mother telling her how much he loved her and that he would be coming back soon.

A few days later, he received a letter from his mother. It said,

'My dear son,

When you receive this letter, I won't be in this world any longer. I know that you will be extremely sad to hear this. I also know that you feel sorry that you were not there during my last days but remember that you are not paying me a great tribute if you let my death become a great event of your life. Don't dwell on the past, and don't let this event determine your future.

I will be watching you from the sky, and if I see you happy, I will feel that my life's purpose is fulfilled. Therefore, if you want to pay me a tribute as your mother, then have a good and fulfilling life.

Your loving mom.'

Tears were dropping from the son's eyes, but they were tears of joy instead of sorrow.

Imagine each phase of your life as an episode of a TV show. You are the main character of this show, with many supporting cast members that come and go in the form of friends, co-workers, and family. Each episode introduces a series of events that work to shape your life.

Can we expect a different outcome if we re-watch the same episode over and over again? Remember that as a result of living in the past, we impact our goals and aspirations as well as those of other cast members—the ones who are putting in their best efforts to support us in each episode of our life. Dwelling on the past also stops us from starting new episodes of our life.

Often there are unpleasant events that happen in the past that are quite difficult to leave behind. We may think about those unpleasant moments repeatedly. Still, it is like scratching at old wounds repeatedly, which will not allow them to heal. We become anxious and afraid that the same things can happen again and ultimately become stuck there.

Imagine if you find the same story of the soldier and her mother on the next page, you won't be interested in re-reading it. No one likes to read the same story twice, even if it is a great story, and many times, we get frustrated when someone repeatedly tells us the same story. By repeating a particular episode of our life, again and again, we cause frustration for ourselves and others who touch our lives.

Have you noticed that when we overthink the past, we become anxious about the future? In this process, we start creating our own miserable versions of the future and feel sad about that too. Don't you think this will eventually lead to contaminating our present happiness with problems borrowed from the past and future? The only way to come out of the cage of the past is by moving forward. So, the next time you realize that your show of life is going into 'Replay' mode, immediately take control by pressing the 'Play' button.

Carry Out Your Duties without Thinking about the Past

In the movie *Kung Fu Panda 2*, the Dragon Warrior Po is badly defeated physically and mentally by his enemy Shen, who repeatedly reminds him of his past. He completely loses his focus and becomes immersed in his past memories. He recalls his father fighting and his mother sacrificing her life to save him.

As he remembers all this, he fights back tears. The soothsayer goat approaches from behind and says, "**Your story may not have such a happy beginning, but that does not make you who you are … it is the rest of your story, who you choose to be …**" As Po is able to understand the meaning of these words, his expression slowly changes as a new wave of memories floods over him. This time, he remembers all the happy times he had with his adoptive father, his teacher, and his friends in his journey to becoming the Dragon Warrior.

He slowly gets to his feet with a heart full of inner peace as he feels no more hatred towards the person who killed his parents. His eyes narrow as he is filled with a new determination to stand up and fulfill his duty as Dragon Warrior and save his friends.

Later, when his enemy Shen asks, "How did you find peace? I took away your parents! Everything! I scarred you for life."

Po replied, "**You gotta let go of that stuff from the past cause it just doesn't matter. The only thing that matters is what you choose to be now.**"

We all feel sad thinking back to difficult moments in our past, problems we've had, or times when we struggled to get the breaks that others seemingly got. This way of thinking convinces us that it is natural to be unhappy. When we think like this, we lose our focus like Dragon Warrior Po and deny ourselves the opportunity to be happy. Like Po, unless we remove the hatred about the person or sometimes ourselves, we won't be able to attain inner peace. Forgiveness is one of the most beneficial tools to prevent us from dwelling on the past. If we learn to forgive others and ourselves, we can emerge from our past as a happier version of ourselves.

Epictetus once said, "It is very little we control. We can't control what happens to us; we can't control what the people around us say or do. We can't even fully control our bodies, which get damaged and sick and ultimately die without regard for our preferences. The only thing we control entirely is how we think about things and our judgments about things."

On this planet, not only are human beings frightened when they face dangers, but all the other species also exhibit the same behavior. The only difference is that once wild animals run away from the threats and are in a safe place, they wander without worrying about what happened. However, we humans are tormented alike by what is past and what is to come. As Seneca said, some blessings given to humans do us more harm, for memory brings back the agony of fear while foresight brings it on prematurely. Humans are the only species on this earth that confines their unhappiness to the present because they drag the baggage of the long past with them.

Stop Feeling Victimized—Everyone Goes through Pain and Grief in Life

Once, in a village during Buddha's time, there was a young mother whose baby son fell sick and died. The mother loved her son very much and refused to believe he had passed. She carried her son's body around the village, asking if there was anyone who could bring her son back to life.

Her neighbors advised her to accept the death and make arrangements for the funeral, but she refused. She clutched her son's body close and kept on uttering for her son to wake up.

One of the neighbors suggested that she should go to Buddha as only he has the power to bring her son back to life. When she pleaded with Buddha, he said, "Go and bring a handful of mustard seeds from a house where no one residing in the house has ever lost a family member. Bring this to me, and I will bring your son back to life."

The woman went from house to house, trying to find such a house. At the first house, when she asked if they had ever lost a family member, the woman replied that her grandfather had died a few years ago. She moved on to the second house, where she found that the house lady's husband had died a few years ago. The third one had lost an uncle, and the fourth one had lost an aunt. She kept moving from house to house, but the answers were all the same—every home had lost a family member to death.

She finally realized that, at some point in time, everyone in this world had lost a family member to death. She now understood that death is inevitable and a natural part of life.

Putting aside her grief, she buried her son and returned to Buddha. She finally fell to his feet and said that now she understood that she was not the only one to have suffered the loss of a loved one.

Sometimes rather than accepting the truth, we think we are the victims. We may not see it, but everyone goes through the same pain and grief in life. We react differently when an event has affected other people's lives. Still, we feel like a victim when the same event affects us. What makes us think we are the universe's special darling who will not go through this cycle? Either we can live in the past, try to make things right or fair or at least understandable in our minds, or accept the outcome as part of God's plan and make peace with ourselves.

When we are stuck in the past, we do not allow ourselves to experience happiness in the present. Sometimes, we even justify our unhappiness by reliving the past. Rather than allowing ourselves to remain enslaved by our past, we must learn to make the most of the present which is in front of us. As Indian Poet Tagore said, "If you shed tears when you miss the sun, you also miss the stars."

It is also good to keep reminding ourselves that, though we are part of this world, the world does not revolve around us. In *Meditations*, Marcus Aurelius reflects on how vast and endless the universe is and the infinity of time stretching into the past and future in order to understand our existence within this broader context. Comparing our lives within this cosmic perspective amid the endless cycles of nature is comparing a drop of water with the ocean. In these cases, it doesn't look right to expect the universe to deliver whatever is our will rather than accepting the will of the universe. Therefore, if we expect the universe to deliver what we want, we will be disappointed most of the time. Still, if we embrace whatever the universe gives, life will be much smoother. Epictetus's notion was that we need to identify the things which are external and not under our control and stop worrying about them.

The other important thing to accept is that changes are part of nature. According to Marcus Aurelius, the things we love are like tree leaves. They can fall at any moment with a gust of wind. Therefore, it is worth being aware that the people we love will disappear from our life at some point.

When Chuang Tzu's wife died, someone enquired why he was not grieving like others. Chuang Tzu replied, "I looked back at the time when she was a spirit. Then change happened, and she had a body. Another change, and she was born. Now there's been another change, and she's dead. It's just like the progression of the four seasons, spring, summer, fall, and winter. It would show I don't understand life if I were to follow others."

Though we don't have control over what the universe gives us or the changes that nature brings, we do have complete control over our value judgments. Things happen, none of which are inherently good or bad, and it's within our power to decide how we value them. As Marcus Aurelius articulates, we have almost no control over anything. Yet, at the same time, we have complete control over our happiness.

Nobody Has the Power to Undo the Past

A man always had sleepless nights thinking about his mistakes of the past. The whole night he will be replaying his past decisions or events over and over in his head, wondering if a different choice might have prevented a bad thing from happening. One night, God visited him in his dream. He pledged to God to undo his past decisions so he could have a happy life. God smiled and said, "My son, stop wasting your time trying to change the past; the only thing denied even to me is the power to undo the past. What's done is done."

The following day, when the man got up, he was at peace with himself. He had understood the essence of his conversation with God and thus received the wisdom to accept the things he cannot change.

If God can't change the past, what chances do we have? Then why do we remain in victimhood, waiting for the past to change, to be anything other than what it was, or to use that as an excuse not to go forward? Don't you think that these thoughts actually create resistance to what lies ahead in the future?

As Zen masters say, it is wise to accept that the past is a dead part of your life and leave it as a pre-condition to immerse fully in the present moment. When fully immersed in the present, we tend to let go of our problems and suffering. However, still, most of us unknowingly replay the past scenarios in our minds, again and again, wishing we could create alternate outcomes. Irrespective of how often we play this game, the hard truth is that the past cannot be revived or changed. Living in the past is no way to live out today; we can't run for any period of time with the weight of our past on our shoulders. At some point, we must leave it behind to live a peaceful life. So next time when your past is troubling your present, firmly remind yourself that there is no future in the past.

Do You See the Present through a Filter of Your Past?

In the main plot of the famous story, *Arabian Nights*, King Shahryar is the ruler of a great kingdom. He kills his wife after discovering that she has been regularly unfaithful during his absences. He becomes a bitter and grief-stricken man, deciding that all women are the same, and starts distrusting them. He chooses to marry a new woman every day, only to kill her the next morning before she can cheat and dishonor him.

Finally, he is married to his advisor's daughter, who tells him a story every night, leaving it incomplete at a cliffhanger and promising to finish it the following night. The stories were so entertaining that the king put off her execution from day to day, eager to hear the end. She followed the same pattern for 1,001 nights until the king had a change of heart and started loving his wife.

Has living in the past become your preferred default mode like King Shahryar? Then it is likely that you may always see the present through a filter of your past. If we have seen our parents unable to get along or get separated during our childhood, when we grow up, we may set that as our default mode. This preferred mode will stop us from having deep trust in our relationship. This way, our whole life, we may react based on this childhood experience. These reactions can also come from a past relationship that didn't work as expected. Either way, don't you think we are behaving like the cruel King Shahryar trying to punish the people who trust and love us for the mistakes of others?

I remember a story of a man who visited Lao Tzu, hoping to find some solution to his worries. When he appeared, Lao Tzu promptly inquired, "Why did you come with such a crowd of people?" The man turned around in astonishment to see if someone was standing behind him, but no one was around. The 'crowd of people' he came with was the baggage of past thoughts that defined his view of right and wrong, good and bad, life and death, which he carried with him wherever he went.

Therefore, whatsoever happens in life, we should not let our past thoughts, which create guilt, fear, resentment, anger, regret, or self-pity, define us today. By creating the accumulation of the past in your psyche, we are only increasing the buildup of bad thoughts. This will eventually harm ourselves and our loved ones. We need to free ourselves from the past by changing our default mode to 'Now' so we don't judge people and situations based on our past experiences.

Are You Carrying Somebody Else's Past?

In a well-known Buddhist parable, two monks were out for a walk one day, one older and one younger. They had both taken vows of silence and chastity. As they continued along the trail, they came to a river with a strong current. There, a young woman was waiting, unable to cross alone. She asked the monks if they could help her cross the river. Without a word and despite the sacred vow he'd taken not to touch women, the older monk picked her up and set her down on the other side.

The younger monk joined them across the river and realized that the older monk had broken his vow but didn't say anything.

An hour passed as they traveled on, then two, then three. Finally, the now quite agitated younger monk can stand it no longer. He asked the other monk, "Why did you carry that woman when we took a vow as monks not to touch women?"

The older monk, who had been admiring the woods' beauty and the birds' songs, replied, "Brother, I set her down hours ago on the bank of the river. You, however, are still carrying her."

We often dwell in the past due to insignificant things like the weight of others' past mistakes, regrets, as well as our own mistaken beliefs. Sometimes, we feel the burden of how other people have acted in ways that are unacceptable. We unknowingly spend time thinking about those actions again and again and lose our present moment.

In our life, whatever we do, it is impossible to control others' actions, even if they are our loved ones. Don't you think that these resentments are a sign of foolishness? Instead of keeping these with us, shouldn't we focus on our actions that will make way for a better future?

Don't Let Others Push You Back into the Past

During one of my overseas trips, I met an elderly Japanese man. One day, during a conversation, I asked him how the Japanese could recover so fast after their defeat in the second world war.

He told me that he was running a small business in Tokyo during the war. The loss had a considerable psychological impact on the people of his neighborhood. They could not accept the Japanese surrender as Japan had never been successfully invaded or lost a war throughout its history.

Every evening during the neighborhood meetings, people would talk about the war. They would discuss their defeat, their mistakes, and what the Japanese could have done differently during the war. Most of the time, the talk would end with people discussing how great the Imperial empire was in the past. Overall, there was no sign of those scars leaving the minds of the people. Nobody was ready to move on and progress; the people were still remembering the bombings and having sleepless nights.

Then one day, during another such meeting, a young man stood up and said, "Enough of those glorious old days and our defeat in the world war. We must leave behind our past and accept the present. Now, we need to work together to prove that Japanese people are resilient."

From then onwards, everyone agreed that there would be no talk about the past in these meetings or at home. The neighborhood worked together to fix the neighboring properties that were damaged during the air raids. These actions helped them to remove sights that reminded them of the painful past.

After that day, they only looked forward, and the whole neighborhood recovered so fast that they set an example for others.

Do you think, like the story, you are also surrounded by people who have a strong tendency to keep reminding you of your past? If this is the case, you either have to stand up like the young man or leave the company of those people.

We don't realize it, but when we go back and forth in the past, we drain our precious energy. Instead of wasting it, if we use this energy properly, we have the power to achieve many good things. When we completely let go of our worries from the past, it becomes possible for us to focus on our present and future. Therefore, don't ever let others push you back into your past. If those people are from your close circle, then you need to have an open talk with them and ask them to stop dredging up the past. We all need to accept that mistakes and imperfections are a part of life, but the important step is to take ownership of them and take measures not to repeat them. Once we stop discussing the past, the new talks can make room for fresh ideas, bringing new avenues of growth for the future. Always remember you are the director of your life; don't let somebody else run it.

Conclusion

In his last book, *Island,* visionary writer Aldous Huxley tells the story of the fictional island of Pala. At the beginning of the story, cynical journalist Will Farnaby deliberately wrecks his boat on the shores of this island as outsiders are forbidden to enter this place. He is tasked with persuading the island's current queen to sell the rights to this island's untapped oil assets to an oil baron.

Farnaby awakens on the island with a leg injury, hearing a myna bird screaming, "Attention!" as the locals help him recover. He is slowly introduced to the way of living there, which he finds very peaceful. He notices that almost everywhere, he can find the birds who are constantly croaking the words "Attention. Attention. Attention."

Later, a local told him that a thousand birds were flying around on the island. The previous king had trained them to remind the citizens of Pala to pay attention to live in the moment. One of the main ideas behind these traditions was to remind everyone not to disregard the present, as we often feel unhappiness due to our tendency to live in the past.

As Marcus Aurelius says, "You only live in the present, this fleeting moment. The rest of your life is already gone or not yet revealed." Eckhart Tolle, in *The Power of Now,* tells that the Zen master Rinzai would often raise his finger in front of his students to take their attention away from time. He will then ask, "What, at this moment, is lacking?" It is designed to take the attention deeply into the now. As it is in the now, in the absence of time, all the problems dissolve. Suffering needs time: it cannot survive in the now.

In the classic Disney movie *Lion King,* when Simba dwells in the past, Rafiki hits him over the head with his stick to test his presence.

Simba asks, "What was that for?"

Rafiki replies, "It doesn't matter. It's in the past."

Simba says, "Yeah, but it still hurts."

Rafiki continues, "**Oh yes, the past can hurt. But the way I see it, you can either run from it or learn from it.**"

So, the next time you are deep in your past, hit the imaginary stick on your head, so you can leave the past and live in the present. As Eckhart Tolle says in his book *The Power of Now*, make now the primary focus of your life by constantly saying "yes" to the present moment. Most of us mostly dwelt in the past and paid brief visits to the now. But to enjoy the moment now onwards, change your dwelling place to now and only refer to the past when it is absolutely relevant to the present.

Keys for
Not Dwelling Over the Past

➢ Accept that the past is over, and we can't change it; overthinking about it will only hurt our present.

➢ Stop blaming others for what happened in your past; they also don't have the power to change it. Blaming others puts us in a negative zone, making it more challenging to live in the present.

➢ If someone in the past has hurt you, the best way to move forward is to forgive them, whether or not they have come to you with an apology.

➢ Don't play the victim game forever as nobody in this world is free from grief and sorrow.

➢ At regular intervals, distance yourself from places and things that remind you of the past.

➢ Spend your time with the people who make you happy, the things that bring you joy, and the places that bring you peace. These choices will help in replacing negative memories with new positive ones.

➢ Plan for today; list things you want to do and goals and keep them in front of you. This list will help you focus on the now.

➢ Practice meditation as it helps you stay in the present.

➢ Accept that some situations are going to end awkwardly, so don't wait for closure.

➢ Healing from past pain can take time, so be patient and stay committed to change.

Commandment VI

Thou Should
Be Content

"Be content with what you have;
rejoice in the way things are.
When you realize that nothing is lacking,
the whole world belongs to you."

– Lao Tzu

Before Alexander started his expedition to conquer Persia, he met Diogenes, one of the great philosophers of his time. Diogenes was having a sunbath by the side of a river enjoying the morning sun and the cool breeze.

When Alexander told him about his plans, Diogenes asked him, "What will you do after you conquer Persia?"

"I will go further for Egypt." Alexander replied.

Diogenes asked him again, "And what are you going to do after conquering Egypt?"

"I will set my plan for India." Alexander replied

Diogenes asked again, "And what after you have conquered India?"

"I will conquer the rest of the world." Alexander replied in frustration.

Diogenes inquired again, "And what after you have conquered the rest of the world?"

Alexander smiled and replied, "Once I am the king of the whole world, I will be content, and then I will relax just like you."

Diogenes laughed and said, "If you will relax like me after conquering the whole world, why not relax right now? Is conquering the whole world a precondition for contentment? I have not conquered the whole world, but still, I am content."

Alexander felt embarrassed. Then, Diogenes continued, "Why are you wasting your life conquering the world only to relax, finally, just like me? This bank of the river is big enough, and you can come and join me with your army. It is miles long, and the forest is beautiful. And I don't possess anything."

In a state of confusion, Alexander said, "Perhaps you are right, but first I have to conquer the world."

Diogenes said, "Your plans will create a nuisance to yourself and others. You will never be content because you don't understand a simple thing—it's either now or never."

Before leaving Alexander asked, "Is there any favor I could do for you?" Diogenes smiled and replied, "Yes, move a little as you are blocking the sun."

After Alexander left, Diogenes said to himself, "He is not even richer than me as I have disdained more than he has ever possessed."

Like Alexander, we often believe we will feel accomplished, satisfied, and happy when we have achieved all we want. We tell ourselves that with the attainment of certain targets, we will finally find peace, but this is rarely the case. One of the reasons is that this list of targets never ends; it's constantly growing as our needs slowly turn into greed. Even if we achieve everything on our list, there may remain an uneasy feeling that something is still missing. Do you know what is missing? It's contentment. When the vessel is not clean, it will contaminate whatever goes inside. In the same way, if we are not content with how much wealth we accumulate, we will feel that it is not enough.

Most of us believe that having more is good. In this pursuit, we consider life a race where we must be the best at everything. So, we continue running in this competition, desiring a fancier car, a bigger house, or more money. The race for the next thing automatically starts when we achieve one thing. As Tal ben-Shahar, said, "We no longer accumulate to live; we live to accumulate." Rather than being in the illusion that acquiring more is an achievement, we need to understand that being self-content is the most significant achievement in life. We must understand that wealth and material things cannot make a man happy forever. In his book *Happier: Learn the Secrets to Daily Joy and Lasting Fulfillment*, Tal Ben-Shahar explains that money beyond the bare minimum necessary for food and shelter is nothing more than a means to an end. Yet often, we confuse means with ends and sacrifice happiness (end) for money (means).

Many of us confuse contentment with the absence of desire or denial of our dreams and aspirations. On the contrary, being content means that we are satisfied and at peace with our present, and we trust that our life's turns have a purpose. It is also about being grateful for everything we have instead of thinking about what we don't have. It helps us to distinguish between what we need and what we think we need. Once we are happy and satisfied with what we have, life becomes a lot more beautiful.

We also need to understand that more is not always good, especially when it comes to material things. Lao Tzu once said, "He who is not happy with a little will not be satisfied with a lot." Having little is not the same as being unhappy. Having more is also not equal to happiness. In other words, happiness is not directly proportional to material possessions. In turn, this greed to acquire more and more becomes the main obstacle in the path of contentment. Acquiring these material things brings some joy, but that joy is temporary. Once we are used to that, the mind becomes unhappy, desiring something else. Moreover, later we get attached to these material things and lose life's purpose and meaning.

Of course, we all require material things, but they are needed to improve the quality of our life and not to show off or to compete with others. The same principle goes with the wealth we are trying to accumulate. At regular intervals, we need to reflect on what is sufficient. According to *Atharvaveda*, the Hindu scripture compiled around 1000 BC - "Money and mansions are not the only wealth. Hoard the wealth of the Soul. Character is wealth, good conduct is wealth, and spiritual wisdom is wealth."

When Chinese philosopher Lao Tzu was once offered the post of royal advisor with a handsome salary, he refused and said, "I am the richest person in the world; all my needs are already provided for." We may not desire anything more than we need when we are content. The abundance of the present is enough to lead a happy and healthy life. Once we are content, we will realize that joy doesn't come from material things. Instead, happiness comes from deep within. It is our mind that chooses to be happy and not the surroundings.

There Is a Purpose Associated with Our Life

Once, a king asked his official painter to capture the moment of his royal procession. The artist worked hard, and finally; the painting was ready. He went to the studio that night to have a final look. As soon as he reached the room, he heard voices coming from inside. When he looked inside the window, he was surprised to see that the characters in the painting were talking to each other. The king said he was unhappy because he was not as tall as his army commander. The army commander expressed his sadness as his armor looked menial to the knights. The knights were disappointed as their horses were inferior to the commander's. The soldiers were frustrated as their weapons were subordinate to the knights'. None of the characters were happy with how the painter had depicted them in the painting.

The artist was disappointed to hear this conversation. Suddenly, he noticed that the street dog in the painting following the procession was jumping full of joy. When the others asked

> him the reason, he said, "I am joyful because I know there is a reason that the painter has put me in his painting. There is a purpose in my existence, and I know this masterpiece can't be complete without me."

Don't you agree that unless we accept that we have a place in the portrayal of life and that the picture can't be complete without us, we can't be happy and satisfied? But instead of enjoying ourselves, we unnecessarily compare ourselves to others like the characters in the painting. In this comparison, we ignore our life's primary purpose and meaning.

Robert M. Pirsig in *Zen and the Art of Motorcycle Maintenance* shares his experience of climbing Mount Kailash with other monks in the Himalayas. The monks enjoyed the experience of each footstep as they had a clear purpose for climbing the mountain. In contrast, Pirsig was just undertaking the pilgrimage to broaden his experience with no clear meaning. Thus, he was unable to enjoy nor focus on climbing. Though he had better physical strength than the other climbers, he struggled for three days. Finally, exhausted, he gave up. The rest of them easily reached the peak of the mountain. Like Pirsig, unless we understand our purpose in life, we can neither enjoy the journey of life nor the joy of achieving goals.

As the psychologist, Carl Jung said, "The least of things with a meaning is worth more in life than the greatest of things without it."

Accept Yourself

> A crow lived in the forest and was satisfied with himself. One day, he saw a swan and thought, "This swan is so white and beautiful. She must be the happiest bird in the world."

105

He expressed his thoughts to the swan. The swan replied, "I felt I was the happiest bird around until I saw a parrot with two colors. I think the parrot is the happiest bird." The crow then approached the parrot. The parrot clarified, "I was happy with myself until I saw a peacock. I have only two colors, but the peacock has multiple colors."

The crow thought he could ask the same question to the peacock, but he could not find one. One day, while flying above a zoo, he saw a peacock in a cage surrounded by hundreds of people who had gathered to see him. After the people left, the crow approached the peacock and said, "Wow! You are so beautiful. That is why thousands of people come to see you every day. I think you are the happiest bird in the world."

The sad peacock replied, "I always thought I was the most beautiful and happy bird. But because of my beauty, I was caught and entrapped in this zoo. I have examined the entire zoo and realized that the crow is the only bird not kept in any cage. So, for the past few days, I have thought that if I were a crow, I would be happier as I could roam freely."

Most of the time, we don't value what nature has given us. Instead, we are envious of what others have. This comparison leads to a vicious cycle of disappointment and, thus, unhappiness. So many times, while comparing ourselves with others, we focus on what we don't have, but deep down, we don't need it or even want it for ourselves.

Like the crow, we forget that sometimes what we wish for can be a curse for us. There is no point in criticizing ourselves or feeling sad, desiring things out of our reach or what we can't change. On a material level, a happy life is no more than a series of goals to be reached, but true peace and stability come from within, from the acceptance of ourselves. Therefore, the first ingredient of being content is to 'accept ourselves' with a sense of gratitude. Once we accept ourselves completely, we will automatically stop trying to become like others. The next ingredient is to accept our loved ones and stop comparing them with others. A person who loves himself and his loved ones has taken the first step towards contentment.

Do Not Neglect Your Loved Ones

The king of a vast empire had a beautiful and loving wife, but he always thought that, as a master of a great empire, he deserved to have the best wife in all aspects. Due to this feeling, he always neglected her. The queen often felt sad due to the king's behavior. One day she told this to her brother who was a great magician.

The next day the magician came to see the king. After a while, he said, "I can see your future. A beautiful life is waiting for you ahead." Impressed by these words, the king was interested to know more about his future. The magician replied, "Oh my Lord, instead of telling you, I can show you what lies for you in the future." The magician took the king near the drinking fountain in the center of the room. He then asked the king to get his head close to the water. The magician plunged the king's head beneath the water as soon as he did that. The king tried to pull his face back, but the magician was very strong. Soon, he lost consciousness and felt like he was drowning. After a while, when he opened his eyes, he saw himself lying on the shore of a strange beach.

He was feeling too weak to get up but then heard the voices of people coming near him. One of them shouted with joy, "See, my slave died yesterday, but God has sent me a new slave."

Before the king could make anyone understand that he was a ruler of a great kingdom, he found himself trudging around inside the treadwheel of a flour mill. The king was tired by the end of the day, but his cruel master offered him only the leftover food to satisfy his hunger.

For the next few months, this was the life of the king. Every day, he would mourn, "I was a lucky king. I had the best of the world, but now my life is miserable."

One day, a boy passed the mill and heard the king cry out like this. The king pleaded with the boy to ask his master to let him go. The boy replied, "The only way to get rid of this life of slavery is by marrying a local girl. Once you marry, you will be set free." When the king begged him to find a local girl, he said, "According to the law of this land, if you want to take a bride, you have to stand at the doors of the public bath and ask each lady coming out if she is married. The first lady who says, I am not married, will immediately become your wife. If you want to try your luck, I can help you get out of this place."

The following morning, the king, with the boy's help, came out of the mill and ran to the public baths. As soon as he saw the first girl coming out, he asked, "Are you married" She replied, "Sorry, I am already married." The king asked each girl he saw, but he received the same response. The king was disappointed, but then he saw a shadow approaching the door. "Are you married?" the king shouted to try his luck for the last time. "No dear, I am not married," came the reply. When he saw the girl coming out, he was surprised to see a big and horrible-looking girl. Before he could say anything, the girl hugged him with open hands and shouted, "Finally, I am married!"

The king thought that marrying this girl was better than living a life of slavery. But the king's fate didn't change much after the marriage as his new wife treated him worse than his previous master. He was forced to do all the house chores from morning till night while his wife would relax all day, munching on food. The king remembered his old wife and how much she loved him and cared for him every moment. Now he realized how bad he treated his earlier wife and regretted his bad behavior.

One day, seeing him deep in thought, his wife became furious and started beating him. When he resisted, she forced his face into a giant water tank. Thinking of his miserable life, he felt it was worthless to struggle. He thought it was the end of his life and lost consciousness.

When he opened his eyes, he felt somebody had dragged him out of the water. He was surprised to see the magician in front of him. "Listen, oh lucky king," said the magician, "Those things happened only in your imagination. I have shown you the life you may have led, the twists of fate that might have taken your happiness, and the bad luck that many of us suffer daily. But none of them are written in your destiny. Therefore, be happy and thankful to God, or he will give you the life you have seen just now."

The king apologized immediately to his wife and the magician for his past mistakes. To always remind him about this, he asked one of the painters to write in big letters in his palace, 'I am the luckiest husband on this earth.'

In *Zen and the Art of Motorcycle Maintenance*, Robert M. Pirsig writes, "Many times truth knocks on the door, and you say, 'Go away, I am looking for the truth,' and so it goes away. Puzzling." In the same way, we often fail to recognize all the good things about our loved ones who are right in front of us. Instead, we always look for perfection in them, and thus, we feel disappointed with the little things. Like the king, we often feel sad about our relationships because we expect a perfect one. But the hard truth is that nobody is perfect; everyone has imperfections, including us. We must accept that everyone in our life has come for a reason, and we need to celebrate it. We must cultivate and work on our relationship rather than thinking the right person is out there. Try to start loving your life and relationship, not the ones you expected to have.

To be content, we must accept our loved ones as they are, instead of constantly comparing them with others. We need to remember that everyone is unique and have different qualities. Once we understand this, we can respect the reality of the present, bringing happiness and prosperity to our relationships. Once we appreciate our loved ones, we can see their best version, which will make the bond stronger.

Never Compare Your Condition to That of Others

Once, a poor man who had never visited a theatre in his whole life received a spare ticket from his employer. As he was pretty excited, he reached the theatre well in advance. Once he was seated, he felt a sense of joy, and he started to see all the other people sitting in the theatre. Soon, he realized everyone present there was better dressed, and they had a better view of the main stage than him. As soon as he compared himself with others, he started feeling discontent. While he was in these sad moods, the theatre started, and soon he was deeply engaged in the scene. Once his active mind started enjoying the performance, he forgot about the people sitting next to him, his surroundings, and his discontentment.

The next day, his friends asked him about the experience and tips to enjoying the theatre if they ever got a chance. He replied, "The best advice I can give you is always to keep your attention fixed upon the performers. Never allow your attention to dwell upon comparisons between your condition and others."

Like the poor man, do you have a habit of comparing yourself with others instead of enjoying the performance going on your life stage? In his book, *The Art of Happiness*, Matthieu Ricard explains that repeatedly comparing our situation with that of others is a kind of sickness of the mind that brings much unnecessary discontentment and frustration. When we have a new source of enjoyment or new material thing, we get excited and feel that we are at the top of our game. But we soon get used to it, and our excitement subsides.

Meanwhile, if other people around us have something new, we become unhappy with what we have and feel that we can only be satisfied if we also get the same. Thus, we keep on running toward acquiring more things and new sources of excitement to maintain our current level of satisfaction.

Instead of finding satisfaction in the new source of enjoyment or material thing, it is necessary to train our minds to focus on our world and our family, the actual performers of our life theatres. So, the next time you feel discontent, start thinking about your family and loved ones so you can track back to find the real purpose of your life and thus back into the stage of contentment.

Never Fill Your Desires till the Brim

Once, there was a king who was always discontent despite his luxurious lifestyle. His advisor asked him to get some advice from the famous sage who lived with his followers on a nearby mountain.

The next day, the king traveled to the sage's place and asked the sage to advise him. The sage said, "I will talk to you tomorrow, be my guest, and enjoy this beautiful place."

After the king agreed, the sage asked him to go for a walk to enjoy the nearby natural scenery. He gave the king a cup filled to the brim with water and said, "This is holy water. It will protect you from the wild animals but make sure not even a drop of water falls on the ground."

After being tired from the long walk in the evening, the king went to bed early. But soon, he found that the blanket was small. When he tried to cover his legs, the upper body was open, and when he tried to hide the upper body, the legs were out. The whole night the king was shivering in the cold, not able to sleep.

The following day, the king went to see the sage when he saw him planting small saplings of fruit plants along the fence of the ashram. The sage asked if he had a good sleep, and the king told him that he could not sleep properly because the blanket was too small.

The sage smiled and said, "How about the scenery? Did you enjoy that beauty?" Frustrated with the question, the king replied, "How can someone enjoy the beauty while holding a cup full of water?"

The sage replied, "The water in the cup represents your desires; if they are full till the brim, you won't be able to enjoy your surroundings. Change your definition of full; only have a few desires so you can enjoy life while holding them. I had ordered my people to give you a small blanket. It would have been best if you had folded your legs according to the size of the blanket. The blanket represents your earnings; therefore, to be happy, you should always limit your desires according to your earnings."

The king was delighted with the advice from the sage and said, "I can now understand my problem, but I don't understand why you are planting these fruit trees. Don't you know these plants take many years until they bear fruits? Why are you bothering to do all the work when you cannot enjoy the fruits?"

The sage smiled and said, "O great king, please understand a simple rule of life. We have got a lot from our ancestors, and now it is our responsibility to make sure the next generation enjoys these. I have enjoyed the delicious fruits planted by someone who grew these trees for the next generation."

Are you like the king in keeping your cup of desires full to the brim? Then there is a good chance that you miss important life experiences as your focus is always on the cup.

I recently met my old college friend after a long time. During our discussion, he told me, "Previously, I was always feeling that I am poor as I was constantly comparing myself with my other wealthy friends." He continued, "But now I feel happy as I have changed my definition of rich." "So, what is your new definition?" I asked. He replied, "If your desires are less than your income, then you are rich. Suppose a person has one million dollars but desires a private plane that is far beyond his reach. In that case, he will feel he is poor, but if a person with ten thousand dollars is happy with buying a second-hand car, he will feel rich." He continued, "Now, I have learned to keep my desires in control according to my income, and I feel rich."

What he said makes sense; you can't keep on stretching the blanket if your desires grow every now and then. Sometimes, we feel it is our right to have everything we want in life. The problem is that we feel unhappy when we cannot meet these desires. Instead of caring for our growing desires, it is better to accept that we can never have everything, so why try to have it all? Instead, we must value the present reality and make the most of it. Embrace the things that are important in life: current time, loved ones, and health.

Being grateful is another important way to find the source of real meaning and pleasure in life. Instead of asking for more and more, don't you think we should be grateful for things we enjoy daily, like the knowledge and arts our ancestors left for us? Sometimes, giving can bring more happiness than receiving. As Buddha said, "Thousands of candles can be lighted from a single candle, and the life of the candle will not be shortened. Happiness never decreases by being shared."

Always Look at the Brighter Side of Life

Once, during heavy flooding, two families were saved by a rescue team, but their houses were severely damaged. After the rescue, one man, sitting apart from his family, was seen crying, looking at the damage to his house. The other one was also in tears, but these tears were tears of joy as he was happy that at least his family was safe and together. Both men perceived and hence experienced the same event differently. One had found his reason to be unhappy, and the other had found a reason to be happy. As Ralph Waldo Emerson once said, "To different minds, the same world is hell, and heaven."

Epictetus once said, "He is a wise man who does not grieve for the things he has lost but rejoices for those remaining." The happy man in the story ignores what is lost but what is remaining is enough to be happy for him. We need to learn from the happy man to look at the bright side in each situation. We can make a conscious decision in any situation, picking up the positive aspect and being merry. Remember, if we look at the negative side of life, we will not even appreciate the beauty of the rose as we will be looking at the thorns.

We need to remind ourselves that happiness is a state of mind, and the positive mind can always find something to cheer for. At times, the sorrow inside us will cloud our minds to the extent that we cannot focus on the joy inside it. Still, the positive mind will filter out the negativity that dampens our mood. Being content is not about suppressing our negative feelings but increasing our positive ones.

Aristotle once said that "happiness is self-contentedness." According to him, to be truly content, we need to learn to be satisfied with every aspect of life. It is often challenging to extract happiness from tragic circumstances, as we usually get attached to tragedies with a series of negative thoughts. But once we understand this is the truth of life from which nobody can escape, we start accepting the reality of life. Train your mind to develop a positive mindset that is not affected or disappointed by external conditions.

Conclusion

There is a legendary story of King Midas, who was not content despite his great wealth. His perception was that more wealth will bring more happiness to him. One day, he was presented with an unexpected opportunity when God asked him for any wish. Midas quickly replied, "I wish that everything I touch turns to gold!" God warned the king to think well about his request, but Midas was positive, and finally, he was granted the wish.

Midas was beyond ecstatic that he now had the golden touch and would be the wealthiest man in the world. Eager to see if his wish had come true, he touched his furniture, and it turned into gold. He touched whatever he saw in the palace until he got exhausted and happy at the same time.

He ordered the servants to prepare a feast. As he touched his food, it turned into gold. Suddenly, he started to feel upset. His beloved daughter entered the room at that moment, and when Midas hugged her, she turned into a golden statue. Despaired and fearful, he now understood that the boon was actually a curse for him. He raised his arms and prayed to God to take this curse back from him. Finally, God forgave him and took the wish back, and his daughter returned to life. In that moment, Midas realized he had enough before but wasted his precious time wanting more. As *The Talmud* states, the one who is content with what he has is a real wealthy person.

The Roman poet Horace once said, "He will always be a slave who does not know how to live upon a little." Sometimes, like Midas, we don't recognize true happiness in what we have and become slaves to our desires to acquire more. We wish for things that we do not require and forget to enjoy the present moment. We can be satisfied, even with very little in our lives, but the minute we're given something bigger and better, we want even more! We work harder to achieve these things without caring about our health and the well-being of our loved ones.

In the forests at the foothills of the Himalayas, there lives the musk deer, which is famous for the valuable scented musk found in its navel. These deer constantly search the jungle throughout their lives for this musk, not knowing that the scent is coming from their own belly button.

We are also like that musk deer, in a constant search for happiness, not knowing that we already possess this most of the time. Unless we do a mental shift to see that what we are trying to seek is already within us, we will keep wandering like the deer in search of contentment.

Contentment is a state of mind that depends little on outward circumstances. When we are in a joyous state, the world seems to be a joyful place. Whereas when we are in a miserable condition, everyone and everything in this world reflects our misery. So, now onwards, make it a point to look inward to what you already possess. Marcus Aurelius once said, "Look within; the fountain of all good is within." The peace and contentment that we are searching for are within us. The moment we understand this, our pursuit of happiness will be over.

Keys for Being Content

- ➤ Have regular retrospectives and clearly distinguish between what is "sufficient" and what is "more" for you. This will help you to differentiate between your wants and needs.
- ➤ Spend time in activities and practices which bring happiness like meaningful work, spending time with people whom you love the most, including yourself.
- ➤ Never compare yourself with others; always remember each one of us is unique and sailing on a different boat. Help others and share the happiness. That is one of the best ways to feel content.
- ➤ Keep reminding yourself that being content is a state of mind that depends very little on surroundings and outward circumstances.
- ➤ Instead of always looking out, look inward and try to improve yourself. This will eventually help you in self-contentment.
- ➤ Keep a strong belief that everyone is having the same access to happiness.

Commandment VII

Thou Should Know When to Stop

It is not necessary to finish or win all the battles,
Sometimes a successful retreat is more
significant than the victory itself.

Alexander the Great became King of Macedonia at the young age of 20. Over the next ten years, as a great conqueror, he amassed the largest empire in the ancient world—covering around 3,000 miles. Nevertheless, this enormous empire was not able to quench Alexander's thirst. He continued his campaign, driving farther east until he reached India and the Indus River; however, the spirit of his army was not with him.

Exhausted by years of campaigning, his army refused to fight further and join their king on his next expedition. Alexander tried his best to persuade the soldiers, but his generals advised otherwise. One army officer, Coenus, finally rose to speak on behalf of the ordinary soldiers. He shared the feeling of the soldiers and their willingness to return home. In the end, he said to Alexander, **"If there is one thing above all others a successful man should know, it is when to stop."**

Not willing to give up so easily, Alexander confined himself to his tent for three days, but finally understood the meaning of these golden words and decided to end his campaign to return home with his troops.

We all know that challenging ourselves is the norm in today's world. Everybody is talking about hustle culture, trying hard, pushing ourselves, raising our bar, and so on. Listening to this, most of us may feel that the idea of stopping or exiting even when things are not working is a sign of weakness. But in reality, it is the opposite; it can be a significant sign of strength as it allows us to sense the current situation and proactively move on. Most of us don't want to waste previous investments and efforts, so we continue to lurk at dead ends. In this journey, we keep on blaming others or playing victim to the problem. Therefore, accepting a withdrawal also shows that we have the strength to admit our mistakes. It allows us to set our eyes on the next course of action, ensuring we are adequately set up to take on the next challenge.

It is crucial to distinguish withdrawal from surrender or giving up. The person who has given up will never try the same thing again and thus will never understand the taste of success. On the other hand, the person who withdraws when the conditions are unfavorable, changes his ways, and tries again, will succeed in the future. Deliberately stopping also doesn't mean a lack of perseverance. Instead, it's an actual assessment of what is suitable for us based on the current environment and circumstances. It also means we are leaving our current situation for a reason with a plan of action. We often need to stop to reflect on what we have achieved until now and check if the goal is attainable or if its persuasion is really making us happy. This reflection allows us to use the energy to check other options and cut our losses.

Have you ever noticed that sometimes in the persuasion of these endless goals, we sacrifice the well-being of ourselves and our loved ones? Having goals in life is necessary, but if they are not tangible, we may make a maze for ourselves with no exit. For example, if we have set up a goal to spend more time with family and friends once we are rich, we will keep pushing ourselves to work more and more. Without a clear definition of rich, we may feel that we are still far from our goal when we see others acquiring new things, like a neighbor getting a new car or our friend buying a new house. In this way, we will keep pressing ourselves to deny the opportunity to spend time with our family.

Don't get under the impression that a retreat is applicable only for big goals, but it can also apply to the small things we do daily to seek pleasure. For example, if we are having a lavish feast enjoying each bit of the meal, but we don't stop at the right time, we will overeat, and this source of joy will result in a source of pain. Don't you agree that what we consider the way of happiness leads to suffering if we don't know when to stop?

One of the other advantages of these 'STOP' moments are they give us time to reflect and gain more insight into understanding "Who we are?", "What do we want to be?" and "What is suitable for us?" It is up to us to decide whether we want to see today as a new start or continue wasting our life because of the time and things we have invested in. While reflecting, don't ever think that the time is gone, but consider it an experience gained and set up new goals based on that experience.

It Is Also a Victory to Know When to Retreat

Chandragupta Maurya, the founder of the great Maurya Empire, unified most of India under one administration and came from a humble background. Chanakya, a statesman, teacher, and philosopher, saw enormous potential in Chandragupta and took him from his adopted parents to train him in the art of warfare and political leadership.

After the death of Alexander, the young Chandragupta led a revolt in the Indian land, which was under Greek rule, and captured large parts of it. Then, he set out to conquer the powerful Nanda Empire that ruled the northern part of present India.

In one of the decisive battles, the vast Nanda army almost defeated the army of Chandragupta. Still, Chandragupta, standing with his men, was not ready to leave the battlefield. His mentor Chanakya advised him to withdraw along with his army. He replied, "Running away is a sign of cowardice; I will fight till death with my men."

Chanakya smiled and replied, "In the situation where the defeat is definite, running away from the battlefield is a sign of bravery, not cowardice." Finally, Chandragupta retreated and hid in the forest with his army for a few days.

After a while, he returned to his kingdom and worked on the weaknesses that caused his defeat. He formed another strong army within a year with which he attacked the Nanda Empire again, and he easily won this time.

Like Chandragupta, most people think they can overcome almost any obstacle if they keep pressing and work hard—regardless of the circumstances, environment, and risks. With this belief, they keep on pushing themselves and others. But wise men like Chanakya know that ignoring circumstances and continuing is a recipe for disaster.

General George Washington, the pioneer of the American Independence War, lost more battles than he won while fighting the British. Yet he was able to prevail and won against the British. He won, not due to his decisive victories, but because of his superior retreats. One of his best retreats was during the Battle of Long Island. After the British landed with an army twice as big as the Washington army, he managed to use the cover of darkness to escape without losing supplies or a single life. This retreat helped him secure victories in subsequent battles.

We need to remember that there is no dishonor in withdrawing to fight another day, whether it is a battle or the pursuit of a new goal. Sometimes, this withdrawal allows room for a fresh perspective to solve the problem. Cutting losses is always difficult but think of it as a chance to reinvest.

Have You Defined the Boundary for Your Weakness?

The Mahabharata, one of the fascinating Indian epics, revolves around the struggle for the throne between two sets of cousins, the Kauravas and the Pandavas. The Kauravas were very jealous of the achievements of the Pandavas. Knowing that Yudhishthira, the eldest of the Pandavas, was fond of dice but unskilled at it, the Kauravas invited the Pandavas for a friendly game of dice.

During the game, Yudhishthira staked his gems, ornaments, jewels, palaces, army, and kingdom one by one and lost everything. Like a losing gambler, he was so invested in the game and carried away by the intoxication of it that he lost control of his mind. Desperate to win, he staked and lost his four brothers, himself, and even his wife during the game.

Being the wisest of men, he lost everything, not only because of his weakness in gambling, but also because he was playing without any exit plan.

This story depicts the fragile nature of the human mind. It shows how every individual has certain weaknesses. If we don't identify our weaknesses and create a boundary for them, we will be doomed someday like King Yudhishthira. Yudhishthira was lured into gambling despite knowing its dangers. In the heat of the game, he ceaselessly and mindlessly increased the stakes. He forfeited each of his material and personal assets, blinded by the hope of some chance to win, but he lost every time.

Yudhishthira was wise and morally upright, yet he fell for his gambling weakness. Therefore, know your limits. Self-deceptions regarding our own abilities can be very dangerous. This depends on the abilities as well as the physical and social environments in which we find ourselves at different times.

Wisdom is essential for deciding not only between right and wrong, but also the boundaries for the choices we make every day. Think of these boundaries as a brick wall you can't cross under any condition. If there is only one thing you pick from this book, let it be that you should identify your biggest weakness and create an exit plan for it. One of the greatest victories in life is being aware of your weaknesses and having an action plan to withdraw when caught up in the situation.

Plan Ahead for Your Exit Strategy

The epic "Odyssey" by the poet Homer revolves around the story of the great Greek hero Odysseus. He is returning home with his men from the Trojan War. During their voyage, they passed the Sirens' Island. The sirens were infamous for luring sailors to the rocky cliffs of their island home with mesmerizing voices that no man could resist.

Odysseus is warned about this danger by Greek goddess Circe. However, he is still interested in listening to the sirens' song. He knew that his ability of self-control would not work when he was under the influence of the honeyed music, so he planned out an exit strategy. Odysseus asked his crew to plug their ears with beeswax and tie him to the mast of his ship. He firmly instructed his men to tie him tighter if he asked to be set free, succumbing to the sirens' song while passing the sirens' rocky islands.

Through his ingenious plan, which Odysseus made while he was thoughtful, he was able to gain knowledge of the Sirens' song without getting himself killed. At the same time, he and his crew safely sailed out without getting trapped by the sirens.

This story of Odysseus teaches us that there are limitations to will power. It is always wise to be self-aware of your will power limits and plan a successful exit strategy accordingly. In the olden days, the wise Romans who knew drinking was their weakness used to plan an exit strategy before going to a drinking party. In advance, they will give firm instructions to their servants to stop serving them drinks after they are drunk and take them away from the banquet, ignoring all their requests.

There is a similar concept of planning an exit strategy in the stock market to prevent losses called stop-loss orders. It is an exit plan to limit the loss on a stock. Suppose we have just purchased a stock at $20 per share, but we don't want to lose more than 10% of the amount. So, after buying the stock, we enter a stop-loss order for $18. If the stock price falls below $18, automatically, our stocks will be sold at the prevailing market price. Placing this order in advance will prevent further losses and detach us from emotional decision-making when the market falls.

Don't you think we need to plan and set up the stop-loss orders for the choices we make everyday? Imagine going to a bar and being aware that you cannot control yourself or your budget after a couple of drinks. In this case, you can set up a stop-loss order like the wise Romans by leaving your credit card at home and bringing limited cash, so there is no chance of overspending. Alternatively, you can take an accountable friend or partner who can watch over you. The idea behind this exercise is to have a plan executed beforehand so you don't have to worry about decision-making when you are not in the best position.

Do you think your decisions are affected due to the heat of the situation? Then isn't it wise to plan earlier so we can better deal with them rather than regretting it later? Planning these strategies earlier also allows our decision-making process to be free from any emotional influences.

Don't Keep on Running for the Unknown Future

Once a king lost his way while hunting. He was helped by a poor man looking for wood in the forest. Happy with him, the king said, "Ask me for any reward." The poor man replied, "My Lord, please give me a small piece of land so I can live and farm there."

Delighted with his answer, the king said, "I will give you the length of the ground you can walk in a day as long as you are able to return to the starting point before sunset."

Early the following day, the man started to cover ample land for himself. After covering a long distance, he thought maybe he should cover more as once he had a family and children, they should have enough for themselves. When tired, he pushed himself for this "once-in-a-lifetime opportunity," thinking about his grandchildren and all his coming generations.

He walked all afternoon; until he remembered that the condition to get the land was to get back to the starting point before sunset. Unfortunately, his greed had taken him extremely far away from the starting point.

He immediately began his return journey keeping an eye on how fast the sun was setting. The closer it came to sunset, the quicker he ran. He was exhausted and out of breath, but he pushed himself beyond the point of endurance.

When he finally reached the starting point before the sun had set, he collapsed and died. Even after walking such a long distance, the poor man needed only a little land under which he was buried.

Like the poor man in the story, we rarely spare a minute and stop to be grateful for all we have achieved. Instead of looking back at the distance we have covered and enjoying what we already have, we stretch out ourselves to cover more and more. In this process, we miss all the fun of present life. If we don't stop and enjoy our life now, we will constantly run the race of 'who is having more' which ends only at the graveyard. Try to be in harmony with your body and never ask more than it can give. We need to constantly remind ourselves what is enough; otherwise, once greed has taken over the mind, we will never be at peace. The mind is a beautiful servant but a dangerous master!

Conclusion

An interesting study was done to understand why people are reluctant to pull the plug and stop even when they know they are drifting towards disaster. In this research, done in 2011 by psychologists Daniel Molden and Chin Ming Hui, the participants were divided into prevention and promotion-focused groups. The participants in the prevention-focused group spent 5 minutes writing about their duties and obligations—a task that has been shown to evoke a mindset of protecting against loss—and participants in the promotion-focused conditions spent 5 minutes writing about their personal hopes and aspirations—a task that has been shown to evoke a mindset of seeking gains.

The participants were then asked to play the role of president of an aviation company that had committed $10 million to develop a special airplane. With the project nearly complete and $9 million already spent, participants were informed that a rival company announced it had created its own plane that provided superior performance at a lower cost. The participants were asked to choose whether to invest the remaining $1 million to complete or cancel the project.

Molden and Hui found that participants who had been prompted to think about growth and advancement were more likely to abandon the project. In contrast, the participants who were led to think about duties and obligations felt they needed to see the project to the end. This study shows that we are more likely to ride the sinking ship if we are hung up on our obligations instead of focusing on our hopes and aspirations. Concentrating on duties and responsibilities makes people feel anxious about accepting failure.

When we see our goals in terms of what we can gain rather than what we might lose, we are more likely to see a doomed endeavor for what it is and try to make the most of a bad situation. This phenomenon of clinging to bad investments applies to a host of scenarios, from explaining why some people stay in bad relationships to why politicians throw military resources into failing wars.

According to Dr. Molder, the greater the resources utilized in a project, the harder it is for people to accept the loss. But if they ask themselves, "What am I going to do next?" or "What should I do with what I have left?" they will be able to move on to better, potentially fruitful endeavors.

So, if you're thinking about leaving a bad job, relationship, or investment, brainstorm all the things you could gain by cutting your losses. Keep shifting your focus to promotion rather than prevention. This exercise will help you see better alternatives and lead you toward a brighter future. Always remember, it is never too late to change your mind. If you discover new information or have an intuition that suggests you have asserted a situation incorrectly, change your attitude or actions, however late in the day. The truth is, it's not where you are now, it's the direction you're heading in. As an old Turkish proverb says, "No matter how far you have gone on a wrong road, turn back."

Keys for Deciding When to Stop

- ➢ When you decide on a particular choice, spend some time defining the boundaries.
- ➢ Believe in yourself but be aware of your limitations.
- ➢ Listen to your body and don't stretch yourself to impress others.
- ➢ Don't compare your limits with others. It all depends on your criteria of success and your value of time.
- ➢ It is good to remember that not every problem is worth solving.
- ➢ When thinking to stop, be positive and brainstorm all the things you could gain.

Commandment VIII

Thou Shall Never Give Up on Yourself

---

*Everyone has weaknesses;
everyone has bad days,*

*Even the legends make mistakes,
even angels fall.*

*As an eclipse can only overshadow
the Sun for a short while,*

No problem can suppress you for long.

*So never doubt yourself and never think
of giving up on yourself.*

Once, a young boy was frustrated with the constant challenges in his life. On the one hand, he found it difficult to survive in school; on the other hand, his teachers and parents constantly scolded him for his low grades, and his friends bullied him. Finally, one day he cried out, "I've had enough of life! A loser's life is worth nothing in this world!" In his frustration, he decided to run away from home.

As he passed the nearby river, he noticed a giant frog sitting on the bank of the river. To his surprise, the frog laughed and spoke, "All the species in this world envy the life of a human, who has intellect, can think, can do, and get things done. Nature has bestowed her blessings on this form of life, and you still think of giving up so quickly!

Just look at me. I don't have hands to clean the dirt from my body or crush the biting insects that drive me mad. With your hands themselves, there is so much you can do; on top of that, you have the power of the brain, which no other species in the world can match. Consider yourself lucky that you are not a frog like me."

The frog continued, "Yet as a small frog, I am happy that at least I have a proper body. Look at those small insects which are crushed when you humans walk. Remember, human life is an achievement. Pull yourself together and go back to face your challenges."

Then, the frog dropped its disguise and revealed itself to be an angel. The boy felt sorry and promised the angel that he would never think of giving up on life again, no matter what.

Like the young boy, we all want our lives to go smoothly without any trouble, but every other day we find some problems that come from nowhere. Mostly, instead of dealing with them, we tend to become our own worst enemies. We think of ourselves as victims and descend into a well of self-pity, promptly sinking into the waters of depression.

Have you experienced that none of these actually help to solve our problems? If this is the case, don't you think that rather than complaining, we should accept that problems are a part of life and the best way to deal with them is to face them? One of the primary requirements for achieving greatness is to accept every challenge in life's path, whether it is a success or a failure. Not only do these failures help us to become firm, but there is a lot to learn from them. Seneca once said, "Problems strengthen the mind as labor strengthens the body." Therefore, welcome and be prepared for the blows that inevitably fall upon us.

According to Epictetus, one of the best ways to handle problems is to view them as sparring partners instead of feeling bogged down by them. Rather than sulking, we should be ready to cherish the challenging parts of our lives because that is precisely when our values are tested. We need to understand that the difficulties and misfortunes presented in our daily lives are not intended to inflict pain upon us. Rather, they are presented to promote strength, provide an opportunity to overcome, and prove one's greatness. Have you noticed that in dealing with hardship, we emerge stronger? Then don't you think instead of sulking in trivial matters, we're better off accepting and conquering whatever might attempt to stand in our way, like a wrestler training for a prizefight? Epictetus once said, "A true man is revealed in difficult times. So, when trouble comes, think of yourself as a wrestler whom God, like a trainer, has paired with a tough young man to turn you into Olympic-class material."

Epictetus later uses the example of Hercules and asks what he would have done in the absence of challenges like fighting with wild animals or with the savage criminals of the world. He might have just rolled over in bed and gone back to sleep. So, he never would have developed into the mighty Hercules by snoring his life away in luxury and comfort. Without challenges, the comforts of luxury cause you to sleep the day away. Every obstacle represents an opportunity for us to prove our worth. Therefore, we should not confuse struggle with pain and try to avoid it. So, from now onwards, whenever you encounter anything difficult, remember that the contest is now, and you cannot wait any longer to prove yourself.

Sometimes there are long-term benefits of difficult situations that we are not able to visualize. Zeno, the founder of the Stoic school of philosophy, was a wealthy merchant but lost all his fortune in a shipwreck. Yet the unlucky merchant later rejoices in his loss, claiming, "I made a fortune when I suffered shipwreck." For him, it was a breakdown that led to a breakthrough as the shipwreck sent Zeno to Athens on the path of creating what would later become Stoic philosophy.

Remember Your Strengths

A great warrior king was defeated by a sudden attack by his enemy. He was forced to hide in a small fort with his men. Soon, negative thoughts started occupying his mind, and he thought of giving up. One day, he asked his consular to write a letter to the enemy king that they were ready to surrender.

The consular felt terrible that his leader was thinking about giving up. As requested, he drafted a letter of surrender but asked the king to check the words before sending it. At the start of the letter, the consular had written all the past courageous achievements of the king. After that, it was written that a man of such bravery was willing to surrender now.

The words of the consular pierced the king's heart like sharp daggers. They hit his pride, and he stood up like a titan and raised his sword, swearing to win against his enemy. He was himself again, and he went on with his brave soldiers to fight successfully.

Each of us is endowed with the strength necessary to fight the problems and find our own destiny, but at times, we might not realize them, or worse, we choose not to put them into action. Epictetus once said, "How long will you wait before you demand the best for yourself and trust reason to determine what is best? We already have all the tools at our disposal. Why are we not using them? What's holding us back?"

Do you know your tools and how to use them when needed? Remember a time when negative thoughts have taken over your mind, and you completely forget to recognize your strengths? You are not alone; like the king, all of us are not lucky to have someone who can remind us about our strengths. Therefore, we need to find a way to do it ourselves. One of the ways is to write down a journal highlighting your achievements, strengths, and even small acts of kindness every day. These can become vital armor against any negative thoughts later.

To make the best use of these journals, you can picture an imaginary switch inside your mind, which can shift your attention from your weaknesses to your strengths. So, the next time when you feel negative thoughts taking over your mind and asking you to quit, pause for some time, and take a couple of deep breaths.

Remind yourself that you have a lot of strengths, but they're hiding right now. Then read the journal to 'find them out'. This switch will act as a circuit breaker, reminding you that you have the strengths to turn off the spotlight from negative to positive thoughts. This exercise will also help you to focus on your strengths before your weaknesses consume you. Always remember the words of Winnie the Pooh, "You are braver than you believe, stronger than you seem, and smarter than you think."

Don't Think You Are Useless

There is an old Chinese parable about a crooked, old oak tree by the village shrine. The tree was large enough to shade several hundred cattle. Some of its branches were big enough to be made into boats. Once, there was a fair in the shrine, and a lot of people came. The famous carpenter of the village, Shih, was there with his apprentice. But he didn't even glance at the tree and went on his way. His apprentice stood staring at the tree for a long time and then ran after carpenter Shih. He said, "Since I first took up my axe and followed you, master, I have never seen a tree as big as this. But you don't even bother to look and go right on without stopping. Why is that?"

"Forget it!" said the carpenter. "It's a worthless tree! Make boats out of it, and they'd sink; make coffins, they will rot in no time; make vessels, and they'd break at once. Use it for doors, and it would sweat sap like pine; use it for posts, and the worms would eat them up. It is good for nothing. That's how it got to be that old!"

That night the oak appeared to Shih in a dream, saying, "Are you comparing me with useful trees which bear fruits? Those trees are stripped and abused as soon as the fruit is ripe. Their large branches are split, and the smaller ones are torn off. Their life is bitter because of their usefulness. That is why they do not live out their natural lives but are cut off in their prime. In the beginning, even though I thought I was a useless tree, I now realize that my uselessness has been very useful to me. Because of my uselessness, I have survived for such a long time, giving shelter to so many."

Sometimes, when we compare ourselves with others, we start to feel useless. We forget to see what we are and thus miss out on our usefulness. Not all trees are the same; some are good for fruits and some for shade. Some may take a few months to grow, and some may take a few years. Some trees dry out during winter, some in summer, and some are created to be tough enough to sustain all types of climates. Like these trees, we humans are also different, so we should not waste our time on comparisons. In the long run, you will always be able to see your usefulness. The key is to keep reminding ourselves that we are unique.

The great stoic philosopher Epictetus was born into slavery. He was crippled for life after his first master broke his leg. But he never gave up or compared himself with others but kept focused on studying hard, even working as a slave to acquire his passion for philosophy. Later, he wrote, "Lameness is an impediment to the leg, but not to the will; and say this to yourself with regard to everything that happens. For you will find it to be an impediment to something else, but not truly to yourself."

Failure Doesn't Mean that We Are Not Suitable for Anything

A farmer tried planting wheat for a few years on his farm and failed every time. In his disappointment, he told his wife that he wanted to sell the farm as it was not good for anything. His wife, unhappy to hear that, said, "If this piece of land is not suitable for growing wheat, why don't you try planting rice. If the rice is not growing well, try planting beans, and even if the beans are not growing, we could try planting fruits or gourds. If our land is not fertile and suitable for growing vegetation, we can use the land for cattle farming. Please don't consider this land useless unless we have not tried these things."

Have you realized that sometimes, like the farmer, we give up after we fail a few times? If we instead try other areas or work on our weaknesses, we should be able to find our way to success. The best example of a person who never gave up is Abraham Lincoln. He failed in business at the age of 21, was defeated in a legislative race at the age of 22, and went bankrupt when he was just 24. It took years for him to pay off his debts. When he was 26, he had to overcome the death of his sweetheart. He had a nervous breakdown at age 27, lost a congressional race at age 34, and again tried the congressional race at age 36, but failed again. He lost two of his sons at an early age. He lost again in the senatorial race at ages 45 and 47. Looking at his record of failures, he had no right to think that he could win the US presidency. But that didn't keep him from trying; he bounced back after each failure. He tried and was finally elected president of the United States at age 52.

To this day, Lincoln is considered one of the greatest presidents in American history. He is the subject of more than 18,000 books and counting. Therefore, never consider failure a criticism of yourself and always keep looking for opportunities or trying in other areas. If we are able to keep the drive inside ourselves like Lincoln, we will be able to overcome all odds. The key is to keep the deep belief that something better is waiting for us and keep on going. Later, you may remember the days of struggle as your best days of learning. As Freud once said, "One day, in retrospect, the years of struggle will strike you as the most beautiful."

Find the Worth of Your Life

Once, a man suffering from frequent nervous breakdowns went to see a psychiatrist. He said that very often, during his low state of mind, he felt that his life was not worth living. He had often considered ending his life by jumping in front of the train at a nearby station. He thought the psychiatrist would suggest going through a program. To his surprise, the psychiatrist replied, "The next time you feel the same, pull yourself and come out of your home, and don't forget to lock the door."

The man was shocked at the type of advice he was getting. But the psychiatrist continued, "Then go towards the train station, cross it and go to the other side of the town. There try to find a person in need and put your best effort into helping them. By doing so, you will feel the worth of your life."

A concept in physiology called 'helper's high' arose in the 1980s and has been confirmed in various studies since then. It explains that once we do a good deed or selfless service to others, we get a feeling consisting of positive energy and positive emotions. These acts of kindness act on our body in the same way that exercise does, releasing endorphins that naturally make us feel good.

We often believe 'the grass is greener on the other side'. In this belief, we always think that others have a better life than us. As our good deeds are often done for those going through a difficult time, the experience can remind us that, in comparison, our own life is pretty good. Sometimes, seeing what is on "the other side" can make us feel thankful for what we have. Focusing on someone else can also pull us away from our self-preoccupation and our problems. Studies have found that people who try to help others experience a reduction in depression and distress and can discover that their life matters. So, the next time you feel low or think of giving up, try to motivate others, and you will feel the same reward. It can be as easy as greeting and smiling at unknown people.

I learned a practice a few years back. Whenever I help someone in need, I write a small chit with details, fold it, and keep it in a folder. Whenever I feel low, I randomly pick a few from that folder. I have observed the powerful effect of reading them in uplifting my mood. It resonates with the saying, "If you give a rose, the scent will remain on your hands."

Channel Your Negative Energy into a Positive Goal

Around the 4th century, in India, there lived a princess who was very proud of her learning. She would often put down the wise men in the king's court with her abilities. One day, while walking by the forest, these wise men saw a very unusual sight. A handsome young man was sitting on the tip of one of the upper branches and trying to chop off the same branch from its base. The wise men immediately agreed that this man was a great fool. They decided to use him to take revenge on the princess.

The princess was of a marriageable age, but she had decided only to marry a man who was wiser than her. The wise men brought the marriage proposal of this young man, saying he is a very learned scholar who is on a month-long vow of silence.

This was a common practice followed in those days, believed to promote purity of mind and speech.

The king was impressed by the young man's beauty and the praises from the wise men of his court, but he asked, "How can we have a debate to test his intelligence?" The wise men replied, "In the debate, we will translate the gestures of the young man."

The overconfident princess was ready to test the young man's intelligence by this method. A debate was arranged where the princess and the young man would only communicate through gestures. Somehow the wise men interpreted all the gestures of the young man to satisfy the princess.

The princess, impressed by the beauty and intelligence of this young man, agreed to marry him. But within a few days, she realized that her husband was illiterate and a fool. So, she said, "I can't spend my whole life with a fool like you," and drove him out of the palace.

The young man got extremely upset and decided to end his life by hanging himself from a tree in a forest. While he was planning to do so, a passerby asked him why. Once he revealed the whole episode, the man laughed and said, "You are proving her right by ending your life; prove her wrong by becoming a knowledgeable person."

The young man understood the message and channelized his negative thoughts into a positive resolution. He decided to go back only after proving that he was more knowledgeable than the princess. He studied under renowned scholars and teachers for several years with this resolution in mind.

Later, he became a scholar in literature poetry and wrote many epics, plays, and dramas. He is known as 'Kalidas', the greatest poet and dramatist India has ever seen.

One of the reasons we give up so easily is that we hold on to our insults and failures. We carry these for life rather than putting them down. These negative thoughts drain our energy and hinder our belief in ourselves. Seneca once said, "We suffer more in imagination than in reality." Don't you think we should try to channel this negative energy into something useful by bringing a positive frame of mind? As Eckhart Tolle tells in his book *The Power of Now*, instead of being negative, become an alchemist, transmute bare metal into gold, suffering into consciousness, and disaster into enlightenment.

There is a famous Japanese proverb, 'Ishi no ue ni mo san nen,' which can be translated as: 'On the rocks for three years.' The proverb doesn't say it explicitly, but the idea is that if you are sitting on a rock for three years, you will eventually melt it. Although something in your life may seem strange or difficult at first, you will end up mastering it if you preserve it long enough. Rather than getting disappointed, we can consider failure a challenge to test our resilience and resourcefulness. Always remember there are no quick fixes in life, and anything of real worth, will necessarily take much struggle and perseverance. Once we accept it as a challenge, it will not weaken our resolve—but will make us stronger as we engage with it.

Success does not have to be fast—what's more important is that one simply does their absolute best and remains persistent. Over time the energy of willingness will overcome each obstacle. Therefore, remember that giving up is never an option as life is a grand game, and we have to play until the end.

Attack Small Problems and You Can Easily Tackle the Big One

During one of his attempts to capture a key fort, a great king of medieval India was defeated by his enemies. He was forced to wander around the forests in a disguise while attempting to stay alive.

One day, around evening, he found a small hut in the forest. The hungry king went and knocked on the door. An older woman appeared, but she could not recognize the visitor as he had disguised himself. The king asked the old lady if he could stay there for the night.

The lady was delighted to have a guest and welcomed him in. She later brought out a plate and served him hot rice for dinner. The hungry king plunged his hand into the center of the dish and burned his fingers!

Seeing the old lady laugh, the king asked why. The old lady smiled and said, "Sorry, please do not misunderstand me! I just thought that you are no better than our great king himself!"

The king asked, "What have I done that reminds you of our unfortunate king?"

She replied, "He tried to take over a key fort, just like how you tried to pick hot rice from the center of the plate. That is why he lost the battle, and now you have burnt your fingers. When served with a plate full of hot rice, you must tackle your food from the edges as it is cooler than the food in the center. From the edges, you must work your way inside if you want to keep your fingers from getting burnt. This rule applies not just to eating habits but to everyday problems in life."

She continued, "Instead of attacking the key fort, if the king had attacked and taken over the smaller forts in the surrounding region, the key fort would have been left defenseless. The great king seems to have made the same mistake of plunging his hand in the center of the dish."

That evening, the king got more than a filling meal in the old lady's hut. Of course, he later captured the key fort after bringing down the smaller ones in the region.

Like the king, how often have you directly taken on the big problems by ignoring the small ones thinking they are not worth your attention? Attacking the smaller problems in life before taking on the bigger challenges doesn't make us any lesser of a person. Instead, they give us strength, motivation, and self-confidence and help us keep going. If we follow this approach, it can help us achieve success in everything we do in life.

The next time you notice that you are bogged down with many problems, try to deal with them one at a time. Focus on just one and try to forget all the others. If you follow this, you will be astonished at how much lighter each of them becomes! Meanwhile, keep celebrating your small wins as they hold the key to your eventual breakthrough.

Plan for Appropriate Rest Points

While working at Westpac Banking Corporation in Australia, I was invited to one of their annual forums. One of the main speakers was the CEO of Westpac at the time, Gail Kelly, the first female CEO of a major Australian bank and a very charismatic leader. During her talk, she shared how she could meet the targets for the bank she had planned last year.

After the session, I got an opportunity to talk to her. I asked her whether she felt like giving up anytime trying to execute such a problematic plan over a one-year-long period.

She smiled and said, "I always considered the target in the plan as a peak of a mountain. I know I will give up if I only focus on the peak in my quest to conquer the mountain. Therefore, upfront, I plan for small, small rest points in between. These rest points allow me and my team to cherish the small wins and have moments to reflect on what we have achieved. These rest points keep me going."

We often see fatigue as a sign of giving up, forcing us to think that maybe it is time to quit. But the truth is that these feelings only signal that we urgently need a break. If we have planned these rest points earlier, there are more chances it will motivate us to keep going rather than give up. The power of progress is fundamental to human nature; therefore, never ignore or underestimate the power of micro-wins and rest points.

Don't you think rest points and breaks in life infuse us with motivation to keep going and keep us engaged in the big goal? Studies have shown that these small wins activate the same brain's reward circuitry, which is triggered when we achieve big goals. These wins make us feel energized and confident and are crucial to our momentum.

This Too Shall Pass

Once, a king came to know about a magical ring. This ring had the power to lift the spirits of any person who had given up. It could bring a sad person happiness. The king asked his advisor to go and find the ring for him.

The faithful advisor immediately went on the journey, searching for this mysterious ring. He enquired almost every person he met during his trip about the ring; still, nobody had heard of such a magical ring.

Over time, the faithful advisor became frustrated. He wanted to fulfill his master's wish with all his might, but he could not find the mysterious ring no matter how hard he tried. He almost gave up when he passed by a small village at night, and it started raining. He went to take shelter in a small hut that belonged to a poor ironsmith who welcomed him.

When he was about to leave in the morning, the ironsmith asked him why he had wandered into this place. The advisor was sure that this poor man wouldn't have any clue about this magical ring but thought to tell the truth. The ironsmith asked him to wait and returned with an iron ring on which he engraved something. The advisor was disappointed at that time, but his eyes lit up when he looked at these engraving. He thanked the ironsmith and hurried to the king's palace.

The advisor finally arrived at the palace and handed over the ring to the king. At that moment, the king was in a sad mood as one of his favorite horses had recently died. As soon as he looked at the ring, his mood was brightened up. The following sentence was engraved on that iron ring: "Despite everything, this too shall pass and be forgotten."

When thinking of giving up, you should never forget that the good thing about bad times is that they also pass. The key is to keep going. As Seneca once said, "Sometimes even to live is an act of courage." Knowing that the tough time will pass can help us better deal with the bad times. If we have faith that the good times are ahead, we will be able to keep ourselves ready for any situation. So, the next time you are in such a situation, rather than getting caught up in the problems, take a step back and try to see the bigger picture of life. Once you are able to detach yourself from the situation, it can help you visualize and see things more clearly and objectively. One of the old Indian proverbs says, "Everything will be ok in the end. If it is not ok, it is not the end."

You Can't Run Away from Your Problems

A worried man had nightmares where a deadly ghost followed him almost every night. The more he ran away from him, the bigger the ghost became. He consulted one of the healers and asked about the dream's meaning and how he could get rid of it. The healer replied, "This ghost represents the problems that you are currently facing in your life. The more you try to run away from the problems, the bigger the problems become."

He continued, "Remember, problems are part of your life; running away will not solve the problem. So, the next time you see the ghost in your dream, try to embrace him rather than run away from him, and it will stop following you." The following night the man had the same dream, but as soon as he embraced the ghost, it disappeared and never came back.

In his book *The Subtle Art of Not Giving a F*CK*, author Mark Manson tells us about Buddha's profound realization after sitting under a tree for forty-nine days. One of the realizations was that problems are a part of life. The rich have problems because of their riches and the poor due to their poverty. People without a family face problems because they have no family and those with family due to their family. People who pursue worldly pleasures have problems because of their worldly pleasures. In contrast, the people who abstain from worldly pleasures have problems because of their abstention. The moral is that difficulties and obstacles are inevitable in life. The more we avoid them, the bigger they appear, like the ghost in our story. Instead, we must strongly believe in ourselves, so that even the big problems lose their power over us. They seem to have power only because we give them our attention and believe they are bigger than us.

Did you know that, for a flying eagle, the greatest obstacle is the air, but if you remove the air, the eagle can't fly in a vacuum? The greatest hindrance is actually the reason for the success of the eagle's flight. In the same way, we also need problems in life, as we can only feel the taste of success after overcoming them. So, from now onwards, rather than running away from problems, be ready to embrace them. Rather than asking God, "Please don't give me problems in life," ask for the strength to withstand them, and you will feel capable of facing them.

Think for a while: Have you ever thought of leaving your dreams as you were not prepared to face the pain of the problems you may encounter in the journey? In the classic book *The Alchemist*, the boy pursuing his goal to find the treasure is dispirited and tells his friend, "My heart is afraid that it will have to suffer." His friend replied, "Tell your heart that the fear of suffering is worse than the suffering itself. And that no heart has ever suffered when it goes in search of its dreams, because every second of the search is a second's encounter with God and with eternity."

Don't Try to Meet Everyone's Expectations

There is a famous story about a man, his son, and their donkey. They were on their way to the market when a countryman passed them and said: "You fools, what is a donkey for but to ride upon?"

So, the man put the boy on the donkey, and they went on their way. Soon, they passed a group of men, one of whom said, "Boy, it is not right for you to ride while you make your father go on foot. You have younger legs."

So, the son climbed off the donkey and let his father ride. Another traveler came along and said, "Father, it is not right for you to ride while you make your boy walk. You have stronger limbs."

The man didn't know what to do, but at last, he took his boy up before him on the donkey. They had come to the town by this time, and the passersby began to jeer and point at them. The man stopped and asked them the reason. One passerby said, "Aren't you ashamed of yourself for overloading that poor donkey with yourself and your hulking son?"

The man and boy got off and tried to think about what to do. They then tied the donkey's feet to a pole and raised the pole to their shoulders. They went along amid the laughter of all who met them until they came to pass a bridge. The donkey got afraid looking at the water, got one of his feet loose, kicked out, and caused the boy to drop his end of the pole. In the struggle, the donkey fell over the bridge, and his forefeet being tied together, he drowned. The passersby watching the scene laughed and said, "You guys don't know how to treat a donkey."

One of the reasons we feel like giving up early in life is as we are trying to meet everyone's expectations, like the father and son in this story. When running our life according to others, we forget the actual direction in which we want to take our life. When we allow others to control our choices, we allow them to be the driver of our life cart, and we end up like a dog leased to that cart. Once our life starts going according to the direction set by others, we stop enjoying our life. We end up resisting and thus dragged by the choices of others. One of the crucial things we should learn early in life is to take control of our life by taking the driver's seat so we can decide the directions according to our true passions.

Have you ever realized that when everyone around us tries to control our choices, we often get confused? Remember, if we try to please one, the other will be unpleased. One of the hard truths in life is that people will never be satisfied with whatever we do, and they will still find faults here and there. In this journey to listen and please everyone, we lose sight of our true selves. Therefore, we must suppress and ignore these noises telling us to do what others want and listen to our inner selves. Remember, our competition is not with others but with ourselves. The people who love us will always accept us as we are.

Conclusion

King Bruce of Scotland was defeated six times after leading his small army of brave men against the big English army. At last, his army was scattered, and he was forced to hide in the woods. He was tired and sick at heart and ready to give up all hope. One day, during heavy rains, he took shelter in a cave, thinking about giving up. On the cave roof, he saw a spider trying to weave a web, but it kept slipping.

Six times she tried to throw her frail thread from one beam to another, and it fell short and slid down every time. With great sadness, Bruce said, "You too know what it is to fail." But the spider did not lose hope and tried for the seventh time. This time the thread was carried safely to the beam and fastened there. After looking at the victory of the spider, Bruce cried and said, "I, too, will try a seventh time!" He called his men together to continue their campaign against the English. Finally, they were able to attain victory. Like Bruce, we often give up after failing a few times. But remember, when we are willing to give up, success is somewhere waiting for us to try one more time.

In his book *Ganbatte!*, author Albert Liebermann tries to explore the secret behind Japan's ability to be reborn again and again from its ashes. One of the reasons for the phoenix-like ability is the concept of "ganbatte," a Japanese term that can be translated as: "Do your best and don't give up." This philosophy is deeply rooted in Japanese culture and its approach to life. The everyday meaning of this term is about the idea of making a persistent effort until success is achieved.

The 'ganbatte' attitude toward life is embedded in the Japanese mantra, "Nana korobi ya oki," which means 'Fall down seven times, get up eight.' The mantra speaks to the Japanese concept of resilience and the insistence that you must get up again no matter how many times you are knocked down. Even if you should fall one thousand times, you must keep getting up and trying again. Unless your mind has not accepted the defeat, no problem, big or small, can defeat you in real life. There is an old saying, 'when you lose wealth, you lose little; when you lose a friend, you lose much; but when you lose your courage, you lose all!' Therefore, never lose your courage. Get up and try again.

I found an interesting thing after reading Charlie Mackery's book *The Boy, the Mole, the Fox and the Horse.* During the conversation, at one point, the boy asks the horse, "What is the bravest thing you have ever said?"

"Help," said the horse

"When have you been at your strongest?" the boy asks again.

The horse replied, "When I have dared to show my weakness."

"Asking for help isn't giving up," continued the horse, **"It is refusing to give up."**

As the English author John Donne once said, "No man is an island." We need to remember that we all rely on others at some point in life as none of us are self-sufficient. Therefore, despite all our efforts, when things don't work, asking for help is the best option and the bravest thing to do. The mystic poet Rumi summed it up best in his poem,

"Never lose hope, my heart,
miracles dwell in the invisible.
If the whole world turns against you,
keep your eyes on the friend."

Keys to Never Giving Up

- ➤ Always remember that there can be no problem in life bigger than you.
- ➤ Have a clear purpose for your goals that guide you as a compass when you lose track.
- ➤ Have a "Wall of Fame" with all your friends and family members' names and photos. This comes in handy to remind you of your support system.
- ➤ Write down your strengths and achievements and visit them regularly
- ➤ Plan regularly for breaks and celebrate the small wins without fail.
- ➤ Invest in good friends. They will save you before you drown in sadness.
- ➤ Have a collection of good books and movies; they come in handy when we need a boost in motivation. They also help to divert our attention from the current problems.
- ➤ Always follow your inner voice rather than trying to satisfy all.
- ➤ Imprint this in bold in your mind: Self-destruction is never a solution to any problem.

Commandment IX

Thou
Shall Respect
Your Time

*Ruthlessly protect your time, never leave
any good things for tomorrow,
as tomorrow is unknown.*

Once, an old man spending his last days in a hospital befriended a young man recovering from a minor surgery. While leaving the hospital, the young man said to the old man, "It looks like you have lived a long life; please share some life advice with me."

The old man smiled and said, "Looking at my grey hair and wrinkles, don't assume I have lived long; I have merely existed long."

Then with a serious look, he said, "Keep my words. Guard your time correctly. Looking back at my life now, I realize that I have not spent my time wisely on things I loved. When I was young, I worked so hard to accumulate more and more money. Due to my busy schedule, I didn't spend more time with myself, my wife, and my children and even lost touch with my friends. I wasted my present planning for the future. Now, all that time is gone. My wife is no more, and my children are grown up and don't have time for me."

With tears in his eyes, he stopped for a while, and then continued, "Please take my advice - never delay the execution of things you love to do. Even if it is a small deed like expressing your love, asking for forgiveness, helping someone, or saying thanks, never postpone it for the next day."

Then he paused for a second and sighed, "I exchanged my precious time to get some extra money, which I thought would give me a comfortable life in the later stages. On the contrary, it is just giving me a comfortable death."

Like the old man in the story, do you often forget to live in the present moment, mapping out what is in fortune's hand while letting slip what's in your hand? You are not alone, as many of us form our purposes with the distant future in mind, often forgetting that the tremendous waste of life lies in postponing things.

This mindset robs us of each day and snatches away the present by promising us the future. With this mentality, most of us live our whole life just planning for future goals, ignoring that the future lies in uncertainty. Have you noticed that when people who recklessly waste their time feel their death is near, they cry to God to give them some more time? They will even be ready to spend all they have to stay alive. It is hard to believe how the opinion of the same people towards time change so quickly. Benjamin Franklin once wrote, "Lost time is never found again." Therefore, never live in tomorrow and waste today.

Mother nature has generously given humans a long life to live compared to other species on Earth so that we can fulfill and accomplish many things. But every day, we tend to waste much of it. We struggle to manage our time schedule and usually fail to finish what truly needs to be done and postpone most of it to tomorrow. Later, when we look back at our lives, we realize that our precious time has slipped out of our hands in procrastination and worthless pursuits.

As Seneca wrote in his book *On the Shortness of Life*, "Let us postpone nothing. Let us balance life's books each day. The one who puts the finishing touches on their life each day neither craves nor waits for the next day. If he has experienced and enjoyed everything to the full, what new kind of pleasure can the next day bring? The next day may add something to this life, but nothing is taken away from it."

Are You Filling Your Life with Unimportant Things First?

There is a popular story about a professor who decided to teach his students some valuable lesson about the importance of time.

When the class began, he stood before them with some items on the table. Without saying anything he picked up a big and empty transparent jar and proceeded to fill it with golf balls. He then looked towards the class and asked the students if the jar was full. They all agreed that it was full.

The professor then moved to pick up a box of pebbles and poured them into the jar. He shook the jar gently. The pebbles, of course, rolled through the gaps between the golf balls.

He again looked up to the students and asked if the jar was full. Again, they all nodded their heads in agreement.

He again turned towards the jar, and this time, he picked up a box of sand, poured it into the jar, and shook it lightly. Of course, the sand moved into the gaps and filled up everything else.

He then asked one last time if the jar was full or not. The students were surprised but responded with a unanimous, "Yes."

"Now," said the professor, "I want you to realize that this jar is your life. The golf balls are the important things in your life—your health, your family, your friends—things that are everything. If nothing remained but only these, then your life would still be full.

The pebbles are the other things that matter—like your job, career, and house.

The sand is everything else. The small stuff and the unimportant stuff. This experiment is to remind everyone that if we put the sand before the golf balls, then there will be no room in our lives for the important things anymore."

Like in the story, are you also in the habit of first filling your jar with sand? Then there is a good chance you might be spending all your time and energy on the pity things resulting in no room for the things that are important to you. First and foremost, focus on the golf balls—the foundation of your life, the things that really matter. Pay attention to the things that are valuable to your happiness. Spend time with your family and friends who care for you. Then set your priorities for the other things that matter, and the rest of the small things like sand will automatically fall in place.

According to Seneca, people value the money and personal property they own and spend it wisely. Still, when it comes to value the time, they use it lavishly, as if it costs nothing. They are most wasteful of the one thing in which it is right to be stingy. Like a true philosopher, he practiced what he said and valued the only thing he could genuinely lose and never get back—his time. Like Seneca, try to spend your time on the things that truly matter to you, such as reflection, bonding with friends and loved ones, and important work.

Sometimes, we may find it challenging to determine what things are really important to us. One of the best ways to find them is by writing your own obituary. It can be an excellent wake-up call that can help you make important changes in your life. It can also help you explore and reflect on the end-of-life perspective, reminding you of what's important. Even think from a friend or family member's perspective what they will write about you. This exercise will help you find the following:

- What's missing from your life?
- If you die today, would you be happy?
- Are you satisfied with the direction in which your life is headed?
- Are you happy with the legacy that you've created?
- What do you need to do for your obituary to be "complete"?

So, what are you waiting for? Start working on your fantasy obituary in which you write down everything you wish to do in your life. Once done, remind yourself you're not dead yet, so get out there and make changes in your schedule to "live up" to your fantasy obituary.

Spend Your Time with People You Care For

A man who had completed 50 years of marriage was asked about the secret behind his successful marriage. He said that he was not a great husband during his early days as he was always busy with his work. Due to his busy schedule, he could not even take time to see his old mother, who was staying alone in a nearby town. Every time she called him, he would tell her that he will visit soon.

One day, while looking for something in his drawer, he saw an old childhood photo with his mother when he was in bed after a fractured leg. It reminded him about all the care his mother had given him all these years.

That day, instead of going to the office, he drove to see his mother. His mother was amazed and happy to see him. They spent all day together and had dinner in their favorite restaurant cherishing his childhood memories.

The next evening, he got the news that his mother had passed away. Next to her dead body, he saw a diary. When he opened it, there was an entry for the previous day. "Today is the best day of my life. I have spent a full day with my loving son cherishing the most enjoyable days of our life. I felt like I had a very fulfilling life." There was no other entry in the diary for any of the other days in that year. He felt fortunate that he had not postponed his plan to meet his mother that day.

He always kept that note with him to remind him not to delay the good things he wanted to do for his loved ones.

Next time you are thinking of procrastinating any good work, remember the words of George Eliot. He said, "The golden moments in the stream of light rush past us and we see nothing but sand; the angels come and visit us, and we only know when they are gone."

Whether we accept it or not, time is a limited resource that is ticking by every moment. Seneca stated, "You live as if you were destined to live forever with no thought of your frailty ever entering your head. You squander time as if you drew from a full and abundant supply with no thoughts of how much time has already gone by." Once we have this awareness, we will realize life is too short to do only what we have to do; it is barely long enough to do what we want to do. Therefore, we need to use every moment wisely, or it will be gone and nevermore within our reach.

Marcus Aurelius once said, "Think of all the years that passed by in which you said to yourself, I'll do it tomorrow, and how the Gods have again and again granted you periods of grace that you have not used. It is time to realize that you are a member of the Universe, and a limit has been set to your time."

Don't wait any longer; make a list of the things that are most meaningful and pleasurable to you and that make you happiest. Every day make some effort to work on them. Given that time is a finite and limited resource, you also need to give up some activities that are lower on your list of importance. Don't hesitate to say "no" to certain things so that you can say "yes" to those more valuable to you.

One of the main reasons why we waste so much time is not because of poor time management but because we think that time is infinite. According to Buddhist philosophy, we need to realize that the body is impermanent, like a clay vessel. The life span of a creature is fixed and cannot be extended. When we are under the influence of an illusion of permanence, we think there is a lot of time remaining. This mistaken belief puts us in danger of wasting our lives on procrastination. To overcome this ignorance, we must cultivate an awareness of death.

Our perception of death affects how we live our lives. If each of us knew the exact number of years remaining in our life, then we would be alarmed to use them properly. As Seneca said, "Expectancy is the greatest obstacle to living, which hangs upon tomorrow and loses today. The whole future lies in uncertainty; therefore, live immediately."

Never Delay the Good Actions for Tomorrow

In the epic of Mahabharat, one day, during their exile in the forest, Bhima, the younger brother of Yudhishthira, was in deep thoughts about how they could get their kingdom back. At this time, a poor man came there from a distant place asking for alms. As Bhima was in his own world, he asked the poor man to come tomorrow.

The poor man became disappointed and went back. The elder and the wise Yudhishthira saw this and was disheartened by the act of Bhima.

He came to Bhima and said, "Congrats, my brother, it looks like you have got victory over time. Are you sure that you and that poor man will live up to tomorrow?"

Yudhishthira reminded him again, "My dear brother, even if both of you are alive till tomorrow, are you sure that tomorrow he will be looking for alms, or you will be in a position to provide him alms? Always remember tomorrow is unknown."

Bhima realized his fault. He felt ashamed of his act of delaying good work for tomorrow. He ran behind the poor man immediately and fulfilled his desires.

According to the Chinese philosopher Chuang Tzu, there's no point in lighting the candle when the sun is out or watering the plants immediately after a rainfall. It's all in the timing! The timing of each deed is, therefore, critical. When the need for these deeds arises, their essence will disperse with time-lapse if not done correctly. What is appropriate today doesn't necessarily hold good tomorrow—especially in deeds like giving, receiving, or discharging one's duties. A little help at the right time is better than a lot of help at the wrong time!

The Greek philosopher Heraclitus once said, "No man ever steps in the same river twice. For it's not the same river, or he's not the same man." Therefore, like Bhima, don't keep on delaying good things for tomorrow. Remind yourself that the best time to commit good actions is now. Once we have this awareness, our thoughts and actions will not delay our good efforts. As the Bible says, "Do not boast about tomorrow, for you do not know what a day may bring."

Conclusion

In the movie trilogy *The Lord of the Rings: The Fellowship of the Ring*, Frodo, one of the protagonists, finds himself completely lost. He has faced struggles he never anticipated on his quest to destroy the evil ring, which has the power to corrupt the wearer's mind. He's confronting despair, evil, and uncertainty. The weight of the responsibility that was thrust upon him comes crashing down.

Deeply disappointed with the events, Frodo says, "I wish the ring had never come to me. I wish none of this would have happened." Then he sees his dead mentor Gandalf, who calmly responds, "So do all who live to see such times. But that is not for them to decide. All we have to decide is what to do with the time that is given to us."

Gandalf's words of hope and loving wisdom encourage Frodo to make the most out of the responsibility that fate has given him. These words give Frodo the courage to stay the course to go to Mordor, the realm and base of the evil antagonist Sauron and ultimately complete his quest to destroy the ring. We're all probably feeling a bit like Frodo at some point because of a situation we can't control and couldn't have anticipated. Still, we need to keep moving forward, and best utilize the time given to us.

In one of the interesting stories in the epic of Mahabharat, the eldest Pandava, Yudhishthira, is faced with a sprite who will not let him go unless he answers the sprite's questions. He asks, "What is the biggest surprise in the world?" Yudhishthira's insightful reply was, "Every day, people see countless other people dying, yet they keep wasting their precious time as if they will never die. What can be more surprising than this?"

We often hear the news of other people dying, yet we behave like we are immortal. It is good to regularly remind ourselves that

167

we are like a lamp standing in the breeze. Death can come anytime and take all our possessions, but our good work for others will always remain in the heart of others. People will remember how we have given light like a lamp by helping and changing other people's lives. 15th-century mystic poet and saint Kabir reminded us that we were born as a priceless gem. Still, we constantly change towards worthlessness by wasting our time on insignificant things. Therefore, ask yourself every morning, "What good shall I do this day?" And end your day by again asking yourself, "What good have I done today?"

Keys to Respect Your Time

➤ Do advance planning to set the goals for the week and block your day in advance for the things you love.

➤ Reserve morning as "me time" for yourself to figure out your core values and planning for the day.

➤ Pause at regular intervals to do the retrospective of your time spent.

➤ At regular intervals during the day, ask yourself, 'What is the best use of my time right now?

➤ Avoid people who waste your precious time and learn to say no politely.

➤ Every month, write your obituary to find out what's missing from your life.

➤ Set time limits for every online activity. Create an internet-free time zone, each day between certain hours.

➤ List out all things that don't matter to you but provide temporary gratification. Create obstacles or try to delay these things as much as possible.

➤ Go on an internet fast at least once during the week. Use this day to connect with yourself and your family rather than connecting with the world.

➤ Reflect on your progress and your time management skills on a monthly basis.

Commandment X

Thou Shall
Be Pragmatic

*Practical wisdom is the master virtue,
the virtue that guides all other virtues*

– Aristotle

In my primary year of schooling, I was selected as a part of the chorus for an important school event. For these events, we had a school rule that we should be in neat uniforms and be at school on time.

On the event day, when we were about to start our performance, I realized one of my teammates was missing. We started without him, but he joined us midway, and to my surprise, his uniform was quite dirty. My school principal was very particular about rules and regulations, and I was sure he would tackle him later.

After the event, all the students were called to the assembly hall. My principal asked the teammate who was late to come to the front. My heart was pounding, thinking about what punishment he might get.

The principal did not scold him but asked him to share his story with everyone. He said, "In the morning, I saw a dog hit by a car while coming to school. I empathized with the poor creature and took him to a veterinary clinic. In this process, my school uniform got dirty, and I was late to school." The principal rewarded him for his actions and told us, "Even though he broke the school rule, I am happy that he acted perfectly as a human being. Always remember there are no rules above humanity."

This was my first lesson in pragmatism or practical wisdom. That day I realized that life is not a game of chess where we have to always go by rules, rather our actions should be based on the reasoning with regard to things that are good or bad for humanity.

Aristotle was one of the first to talk about practical wisdom in his work *Nicomachean Ethics*. He believed that in order to make the right decisions, in addition to abstract wisdom, we need practical wisdom. According to him good rules might be useful as guides, but they will never be subtle enough and nuanced enough to apply in each situation. He recognized that balancing acts like these require practical wisdom that uses your knowledge and discernment to do it in the right way. As John Bradshaw said, **"*Practical wisdom* is the ability to do the right thing, at the right time, for the right reason."**

We must understand that practical wisdom is not there to replace the rule book. Instead, it is to enhance and complement it by serving as the method for making the right decision according to the situation. Aristotle said, "We praise and blame all men with regard to their purpose rather than with regard to their actions." Therefore, we need to consider the person's underlying intention rather than what has actually taken place. This is why Aristotle contemplated practical wisdom as the master virtue that made all the other virtues possible. Without the correct application of practical wisdom, the other virtues or good qualities would be lived too much or too little and may turn into vices or bad qualities.

Nothing in This World Is above Humanity

Once, a teacher taught a lesson on truthfulness from the scriptures. After finishing, he asked the students how they would apply today's learning in life. Almost all of them replied that they would now refrain from lying.

The teacher smiled and said, "Let me share two stories; in the first one, a man took a vow to always speak the truth, and he became famous in that village as a truth-teller. One day, some people ran past his house and entered a nearby wood. They were pursued by the murderers who arrived afterwards. The murderers knew about the man's vow and asked him which way their victims had gone. He immediately told them their victims were behind the trees in the woods. The murderers followed them in the woods and killed them all."

The teacher continued, "The second story is about a village boy. One day he was collecting firewood in the woods when he saw a baby dear and his mother running towards a trail. Soon, they were followed by the king and his men who were there for hunting. After looking at the boy, the king asked, "Did you see which way my prey went?" The boy immediately pointed him in the opposite direction, and the king and his men went in the wrong direction looking for the deer. Now, tell me from both these stories who adhered to truthfulness?"

The teacher smiled at the confused students and continued, "Never go with the narrow interpretation of the truth as refraining from lying. The definition of truth is not always fixed. Being honest may not be a virtue when an innocent life is at stake. Truthfullness is about doing the 'right' thing. Therefore, always be pragmatic while following the instructions of the religious books or scriptures."

In his book *Memorabilia*, Xenophon, the student of Socrates, shares the story of the Greek hero Hercules standing at a crossroads of two roads that diverge in the wood. The hero is forced to choose between two maidens, one representing virtue and the other vice - One a life of virtuous hard work and the other of laziness. The maiden representing virtue says, "Make your body the servant of your mind, and train it with toil and sweat, but in the end, there lies a glorious life." And then the maiden representing vice smiles and says, "Don't you see the long and hard life to the joy she is describing? Come the easy way with me!"

Have you noticed that in real life, we often stand at the same crossroads as Hercules? Moreover, the choices are more complicated, as the choice that appears to be a virtue turns out to be a vice, and the vice turns out to be the real virtue. The abstract wisdom and knowledge learned from books can further confuse us rather than help us differentiate between them. For example, abstract wisdom regards truthfulness as a virtue, and we may think to follow it blindly under all the conditions. But like the story, when an innocent life is at stake, the truth may not be a virtue, but it is the opposite; lie becomes a virtue.

In some cases, the decision requires choosing between different virtues, like when your partner or friend asks you, "How do I look?" In this case, you have to decide which of your obligation- honesty or kindness effectively trumps the other. According to Aristotle, even the extreme of virtues is also not good; therefore, we need to always look for a 'middle' path.

Practical wisdom demands that we use more empathy, personal judgment, and wisdom of experience in our daily decision-making tasks rather than blindly following the rules. When faced with these situations, the first question you need to ask yourself is, what is righteousness in this situation? What is the use of these rules and rituals if it is not for humanity or the common good? Acting wisely demands that we be guided by the proper aims or goals for each activity.

Righteous Actions

Jesus Christ and his disciples journeyed to Jerusalem to celebrate a festival. They found the sacred city of God overflowing with thousands of pilgrims from all parts of the world.

Entering the temple, he saw the merchants' selling cattle, sheep, and doves for sacrifices; he also saw dealers at tables exchanging foreign money.

Jesus got angry and cried in a fury,

"What are you doing?

You have turned my Father's house into a marketplace!

Get these things out of here!

Shame on you!"

Then he drove them out of the Temple.

In this story, Jesus took a tough stand opposite to his usual character, but his anger was righteous. Righteous anger springs forth from a sense of justice, a moral compass of right and wrong, and a desire for things to be made right. When it is about injustice, corruption, or the mistreatment of others, we have to show our anger and raise our voice rather than renouncing anger or guarding our tongue. Would you not get angry or speak seeing a weak person getting injustice or the ill-treatment of an animal? In these situations where there is unfairness of any kind, bullying, persecution, or discrimination, it is right to get angry and protest against these acts without breaking the law of the land. Anger becomes righteous when you use it to defend the rights of another without nursing any selfish motive.

In this world, many people take forgiveness and calmness as a sign of weakness. So, even though you are good at managing your anger in certain situations, it is pragmatic to use anger for a righteous reason.

If the Aims Are Bad, Greater Skill Implies a Greater Evil

During the second world war, an intelligent German engineer worked long hours to finish a project. He told his mother he was working on a secret project for the Nazi army. A few months after completing his project, one day, he returned home with an award received for excellence in his work.

That day his mother took courage and asked him about the project. He murmured slowly, "We were working on the gas chambers. I was the one who solely designed those chambers." His mother had read the stories of how these gas chambers were used in the concentration camps to kill innocent Jews.

She replied in distress, "I would be happier if you had not used your intelligence to design such an inhuman machine. I am unfortunate to see how many people have suffered because of your excellence."

How can one be virtuous and yet pursue the wrong aim? In this story, the German engineer exhibits excellence in his work, but he has used his good for the wrong cause. Such an individual may feel torn between loyalty to his duty and his country and injustice to humanity. But he has to think about which good is more important: love for the country and duty or a sense of justice. This is why Aristotle said practical wisdom is the master virtue that can help us match the right virtue to the right moment. In these cases, discernment and reason must determine what is 'right'. We should understand that practical wisdom is the combination of moral will and moral skill. A wise person should know how to use both of these together to serve the right aims, rather than using them to manipulate or harm other people. In daily life examples, we must be pragmatic rather than stick mindlessly to following our duties. Sometimes we must do what seems necessary as a temporary expedient even if it does not lead to excellence. We are born with an inner compass, and we always need to ensure our self-interest is not overriding that.

In her book *Eichmann in Jerusalem: A Report on the Banality of Evil*, Hannah Arendt argues that German officials justified their role in the Holocaust by telling themselves that they were just following their superiors' orders. Rather than questioning them, they obeyed the rules, believing they were not part of the evil. Nazi army colonel Eichmann detached his actions from the end during his trial. For him, once the trains filled with Jews left the station, they were someone else's problem as Maxwell A. Cameron said severe problems arise when agents are motivated only by the rule. Every rule has an exception, and no rule should be more important than preserving harmony and justice in society.

Be Practical

Once, a scholar was crossing a river in a small boat along with a boatman. It was the beginning of the rainy season. The boatman set sail, and the boat was advancing smoothly. The scholar broke the silence and asked the boatman, "How long have you been doing this work?" The boatman replied softly, "Since I was a small boy." The scholar said, "Then you must know all the science about how the boat floats."

Completely surprised, the boatman replied, "I have never thought about it." The scholar laughed and remarked, "What is the use of doing this work when you don't know the science behind it?" Then he started boasting about all he had read from the books about the science of swimming, the principle of Archimedes, and the law of gravitation. The boatman was silently listening to his talk, looking at the sky.

Suddenly, the sky became covered with dark clouds, and the wind began to blow in the form of a storm. The scholar was frightened when the boat started rocking from side to side. This time the boatman said to him, "It looks like the boat will capsize soon now. As you know everything about swimming, you must be skilled in that." The scared scholar replied in a pitiful voice, "I have read many books on swimming and know a lot about it, but I have never tried swimming." As he prepared to swim, the boatman commented, "What is the use of having all that knowledge if you cannot apply it in real life?"

Don't you think that we need to be more practical in life? As the Stoic philosopher, Aristo argued that the expertise of the javelin thrower in the Olympic Games comes from training and practice, not from studying the target or memorizing rules. They get better and better by practicing with the javelin. "One who has trained himself for life as a whole," he said, "does not need to be advised on specifics." Like the athlete, the excellence of practical wisdom also comes from practice. Aristotle once said, "Moral excellence comes about as a result of habit. We become just by doing just acts, temperate by doing temperate acts, brave by doing brave acts." So, we need to practice and train until the skill becomes our second nature.

Aristotle firmly believed that the same principal goes for practical wisdom, which could only be gained through experience, not by just accumulating knowledge from books. He further states that practical wisdom results from experience linking to a skill like carpentry. He argued that we can't just read a book about carpentry and expect to become master carpenters. We have to start working with tools and wood to do that. Similarly, we become more and more practically wise as we make decisions and learn from our experiences. Getting our degree in practical wisdom requires enrollment in the school of hard knocks, as the issues we face are embedded in our everyday work and are not hypotheticals or being taught in our school or university courses.

Once I read a story about a general who was given a thick book after taking over an important command. This book was written by a previous general on choosing the strategies when faced with an attack. The general laughed and spoke, "Burn them, when the enemy attacks, we don't have time to choose. We've to decide immediately, which comes from our own experience." Don't you agree that we hardly remember the rules we have studied in times of difficult situations? During those times, we don't pore over rules; we automatically do it.

Conclusion

In their book *Practical Wisdom: The Right Way to Do the Right Thing*, Schwartz and Sharpe outline that Aristotle was very interested in watching how the craftsmen around him worked. He was impressed at how they would improvise novel solutions to problems they had never anticipated. He got fascinated with how stone masons on the Isle of Lesbos used rulers while carving round pillars from slabs of stone. Their straight-edge rulers proved useless as they could not measure the circumference of the columns. So, they fashioned a new tool—a flexible ruler which can be wrapped around the columns—the forerunner of today's tape measure.

Aristotle recognized that in order to do their work well, the artisans needed to bend the rules. They didn't bend the rules to cheat or deceive. They bent the rules to do what is right and to do it well. Aristotle argued that in the same way, sometimes doing the right thing requires knowing when and how to bend the rules using practical wisdom.

Like Aristotle, we need to understand that choices are rarely black-and-white, and we can't just apply rules to solve them. Our decisions can never be derived from a set of clear-cut rules and principles. That is why practical wisdom is required. Without practical wisdom, it would be impossible to judge how we can use other virtues in the right way, at the right time, or in the right disposition. The knowledge and skill that practical wisdom demands come from both reason and experience. Acting wisely also demands that we be guided by the proper aims or goals of a particular activity.

Maxwell Cameron, in *Political Intuitions and Practical Wisdom: Between Rules and Practice*, shares one of his experiences. One day,

182

walking through the park, he saw a child throwing stones directly in the air. He sensed that the stone might fall back and strike the child but thought as the parents were around, if he tried to correct the child, they might object that it was none of his business. Later, when he saw the kid with blood streaming from his face, he realized that he had not done a good job. He failed to balance between two goods: the desire to protect a child and the concern of being meddlesome. That day, he created a maxim: "When kids are in harm's way, err on the side of protecting them."

Don't you think, like Maxwell, we need to create maxims for our life, believing that affinity for the common good is our primary obligation? So, from now onwards, always try to be pragmatic, ensuring your choices are made considering others, family, society, and humanity. As Marcus Aurelius said, "What's good for the hive is good for the bee."

Keys to Being Pragmatic

- ➢ Don't be passive in following the rules. Always reflect on internal questions like, "What am I doing?", "What is the proper aim of this activity or rule?"
- ➢ Remember, every rule has an exception as long as it is for society's welfare and not for self-motive.
- ➢ To make wise decisions, we need to always take the perspective of others and try to understand their feelings with a sense of empathy.
- ➢ Take the village concept approach to the problem. Think about the other people who may be affected because of your decision.
- ➢ Test your assumptions by asking yourself, "What don't I know right now?" or "What could be done differently."
- ➢ Use the golden rule of always treating others as you would like others to treat you.

Sources Consulted And Further Reading

- *De Ira (On Anger)*, Seneca
- *On the Shortness of Life*, Seneca
- *Meditations*, Marcus Aurelius
- *Discourses*, Epictetus
- *Apology*, Plato
- *Republic*, Plato
- *The Upanishads*, Swami Paramananda
- *Fables and Proverbs from Sanskrit*, Charles Wilkins
- *Mahabharata*, Ved Vyas
- *Think Like a Monk: Train Your Mind for Peace and Purpose Every Day*, Jay Shetty
- *The Power of Now: A Guide to Spiritual Enlightenment*, Echkhart Tolle
- *Aristotle's Way: How Ancient Wisdom Can Change Your Life*, Edith Hall
- *Happiness: A Guide to Developing Life's Most Important Skill*, Matthieu Ricard
- *Zen and the Art of Motorcycle Maintenance: An Inquiry into Values*, Robert M. Pirsig
- *The Tao Made Easy: Timeless Wisdom to Navigate a Changing World*, Alan Cohen
- *Happier: Learn the Secrets to Daily Joy and Lasting Fulfillment*, Tal Ben-Shahar
- *The Boy, the Mole, the Fox, and the Horse*, Charlie Mackesy
- *The Alchemist*, Paulo Coelho
- *The Subtle Art of Not Giving a F***: A Counterintuitive Approach to Living a Good Life*, Mark Manson

- *Ganbatte!*, Albert Liebermann
- *Kindfulness: Be a True Friend to Yourself with Mindful Self-compassion*, Padraig O'Morain
- *Chuang Tzu: Taoist Philosopher and Chinese Mystic*, Herbert A. Giles
- *The Complete Prose Works of Ralph Waldo Emerson*, Ralph Waldo Emerson
- *A Physical Interpretation of the Universe: The Doctrines of Zeno the Stoic*, H.A.K. Hunt
- *How to Be a Stoic: Using Ancient Philosophy to Live a Modern Life*, Massimo Pigliucci
- *Anger: Taming a Powerful Emotion*, Gary Chapman
- *Master Your Emotions*, Thibaut Meurisse
- *The Biology of Belief*, Bruce Lipton
- *How to Think Like a Roman Emperor: The Stoic Philosophy of Marcus Aurelius*, Donald Robertson
- *Political Institutions and Practical Wisdom: Between Rules and Practice*, Maxwell A. Cameron
- *Practical Wisdom: The Right Way to Do the Right Thing*, Barry Schwartz and Kenneth Sharpe
- *Notes on the Nicomachean Ethics of Aristotle*, J. A. Stewart
- *Native American Ghost Stories*, Darren Zenko & Amos Gideon
- *Chapters from Aristotle's Ethics*, J.H. Muirhead
- *Stoic and Epicurean*, R. D. Hicks
- *Ikigai: The Japanese Secret to a Long and Happy Life*, Héctor García, Francesc Miralles
- *Focus Perspective on Sunk Costs*, Daniel Molden and Chin Ming Hui
- *An Open Gate, the World to Come and Speech*, Rachmiel Tobesman
- *Eichmann in Jerusalem: A Report on the Banality of Evil*, Hannah Arendt